Positive Stories

Five Plays f
Perform in R

Robbie Gordon, Sabrina Mahfouz, Jack Nurse, Stef Smith, Chris Thorpe and Bea Webster

Edited by Wonder Fools

methuen | drama

LONDON • NEW YORK • OXFORD • NEW DELHI • SYDNEY

METHUEN DRAMA
Bloomsbury Publishing Plc
50 Bedford Square, London, WC1B 3DP, UK
1385 Broadway, New York, NY 10018, USA

BLOOMSBURY, METHUEN DRAMA and the Methuen Drama logo are
trademarks of Bloomsbury Publishing Plc

First published in Great Britain 2020

A catalogue record for this book is available from the British Library.

A catalog record for this book is available from the Library of Congress.

ISBN: PB: 978-1-3502-3336-2
ePDF: 978-1-3502-3337-9
ePub: 978-1-3502-3338-6

Series: Plays for Young People

Typeset by Mark Heslington Ltd, Scarborough, North Yorkshire
Printed and bound in the United States of America

To find out more about our authors and books visit
www.bloomsbury.com and sign up for our newsletters.

Positive Stories for Negative Times

Presented by Wonder Fools in association
with Traverse Theatre

Supported by SCVO Wellbeing Fund, Garfield Weston
Foundation, Foundation Scotland Response Fund, The
Brunton, Renfrewshire Leisure and Future Paisley.

Wonder Fools would also like to thank Eilidh Nurse,
Gemma Nicol and Lisa Williamson for their hard work in
getting this project off the ground, and the Wonder Fools
board: Vikki Doig, Dominic Hill, Anne McCluskey,
Gary McNair and Nima Sene for their endless
encouragement and advice.

Positive Stories for Negative Times was first produced as an
online participatory project for Wonder Fools, 26 August
2020 to 31 March 2021.

Contents

ABOUT THE PROJECT

Positive Stories for Negative Times is a new national participatory project by Wonder Fools. This innovative and exciting project responds to the lack of physical spaces for young people to participate in creative activities due to the coronavirus pandemic of 2020, and instead allows them to come together to make new work online or live in the space, if government guidelines allow.

Wonder Fools have commissioned some of the UK's most exciting voices to write new plays for young people including Sabrina Mahfouz, Stef Smith, Chris Thorpe, Bea Webster and Robbie Gordon and Jack Nurse. The plays are written specifically to be performed remotely or socially distanced and will be free to participating groups between the ages of eight and twenty-five, from August 2020 to March 2021. Participating groups are sent a handbook of exercises to help explore the play of their choice, and are invited to record and upload their performance to our interactive map which will share and celebrate all the brilliant work from young people across the UK and beyond.

If you are reading this book before 31 March 2021 then you can read all five plays and our handbook at your leisure. If you'd like to perform them then we'd invite you to take part in the project. You can find more information, sign up and see performances from the hundreds of other groups taking part at www.positiviestories.scot.

EDITORS' NOTE

Positive Stories for Negative Times started life in our living rooms in Spring 2020 during the national lockdown. We wanted to find ways for young people to still be creative and connect with one another during a time when we were all forced to be apart. Over a whirlwind couple of months, thanks to the brilliance of the team around us and the playwrights involved, we managed to pull together a project that we hope fulfils these aims.

We are absolutely delighted to have had the privilege of working with such a brilliant selection of writers who are some of our favourite voices working in the UK today. The biggest 'pinch me' moment of our careers so far was when Sabrina Mahfouz, Stef Smith, Chris Thorpe and Bea Webster agreed to take part in this project and we can't thank them enough. The plays are all incredibly different but equally full of interesting stories, exciting forms and searching questions about this extraordinary moment we are living through.

We imagine, though, that the most excitement we'll feel about the project hasn't happened yet. That'll start in the coming weeks when the interactive website begins to be busy with content and the map becomes populated with all the different pins from Falkirk to Falmouth, from Coatbridge to Cardiff and from who knows where after that. It'll be a complete buzz to see what everyone comes back with and the positivity, creativity and connection that everyone will hopefully feel from participating. We cannae wait.

Steph, Jack and Robbie aka Wonder Fools

September 2020

www.positivestories.scot

WONDER FOOLS

ABOUT WONDER FOOLS

'*Fiercely curious Glasgow-based Wonder Fools company*'
The Herald

Wonder Fools are a theatre company that create contemporary new work based on a diverse range of current and historical real-life stories. During our short history, we have sought unknown and forgotten stories lost in the evolving social landscape of Britain that we are able to reshape and make theatre from. From these stories we take theatre productions, performance installations and workshops to people across Scotland and the UK, as well as creating digital work online.

To date we have staged four full productions: *McNeill of Tranent: Fastest Man in the World* (2014/2015), an autobiographical show performed by retired athlete George McNeill, who in 1972 was the fastest man in the world despite never being allowed to compete in the Olympic or Commonwealth Games; *The Coolidge Effect* (2016–present), an interactive performance that examines how pornography affects our mental health, relationships and sexual experiences using a blend of storytelling, poetry and science; *Lampedusa* (2017) by Anders Lustgarten, exploring the acts of human kindness behind the headlines of the migrant crisis and *549: Scots of the Spanish Civil War* (2018–2019), telling the true stories of four miners from Prestonpans who volunteered as part of the International Brigade.

Stories to Connect Us is a season of digital work produced throughout 2020 and includes brand new projects (*Home Made* and *The New Normal*) and our most excitingly relevant previous productions reimagined and repurposed for now

(*The Coolidge Effect* and *549: Scots of the Spanish Civil War*). The season is a collection of stories that examine the past, the present and the future in ways that we hope will reveal something about who we are at this moment in time. In contrast to our collective isolation and to counter our shared anxiety, we hope *Stories to Connect Us* pulls people closer together through the underlying themes of connection, compassion and hope.

wonderfools.org

Twitter: @wonder_fools
Facebook: @wonderfoolsonline
Instagram: @wonder_fools_online

SUPPORT US

Wonder Fools SCIO (SC047673) is a registered charity and arts organisation.

Wonder Fools depends upon the generosity of individuals like you to make our work, on stage and off, happen. For example, Positive Stories for Negative Times could not have happened without the generous and wide-ranging support of organisations, individuals, charities, trade unions and the public.

We would love to run Positive Stories for Negative Times again in the future, hopefully as an annual initiative, and if you find value in the process and you have a little bit of cash to spare a donation it would go a long way to making this happen.

Visit *www.wonderfools.org/donate* to contribute to our work and other projects similar to this one. Together, with your help, we can continue to take our work to young people and audiences across Scotland and beyond.

WONDER FOOLS TEAM

Robbie Gordon Co-Founder
Jack Nurse Co-Founder
Steph Connell Producer
Gemma Nicol (hidden route) Participation Associate
Lisa Williamson (hidden route) Participation Associate
Eilidh Nurse Assistant Producer

ABOUT TRAVERSE THEATRE COMPANY

As Scotland's new writing theatre, the Traverse Theatre is a dynamic centre for performance, experience and discovery. Enabling people across society to access and engage with theatre is our fundamental mission.

Our year-round programme bursts with new stories and live performances that challenge, inform and entertain. We empower artists and audiences to make sense of the world today, providing a safe space to question, learn, empathise and – crucially – encounter different people and experiences. We commission, produce and programme for existing and future audiences to offer new and exciting experiences for everyone, and our partnerships with other theatre companies and festivals enable us to present a wide range of innovative performances.

We are passionate about developing talent and embracing the unexplored, working with the newest and rawest talent – with an emphasis on the Scottish-based – and nurturing it to become the art, artists and performances that can be seen on our stages through a variety of creative learning and literary programmes.

The timely, powerful stories that start life on our stages have global impact, resulting in dozens of tours, productions and translations. We are critically acclaimed and recognised the world over for our originality and artistic risk, which we hope will create some of the most talked-about plays, productions, directors, writers and actors for years to come.

traverse.co.uk

CREATIVE TEAM BIOGRAPHIES

CORE TEAM

Robbie Gordon – Project Lead and Playwright

Robbie is a graduate of the Royal Conservatoire of Scotland and co-founder of Wonder Fools.

His work is socially engaged, embedded in communities and always strives to start a conversation. He currently works as the Associate Director of Creative Learning at the Gaiety Theatre, the Creative Producer for Class Act at the Traverse Theatre and the director of the Royal Conservatoire of Scotland Young Company.

Selected credits: writer, performer and movement director of *549: Scots of the Spanish Civil War* (Wonder Fools); writer and performer of *The Coolidge Effect* (Wonder Fools); writer and director of *McNeill of Tranent: Fastest Man in the World* (Wonder Fools); actor in *Charlie Sonata* (Royal Lyceum Theatre); director of *Open Your Lugs* (Ayr Gaiety); associate director of *Square Go* (Francesca Moody Productions); workshop leader and sand artist on Danny Boyle's *Pages of the Sea* (National Theatre of Scotland); research assistant on *Locker Room Talk* (Traverse Theatre); and assistant director on Graham McLaren's *Dream On!* (Royal Conservatoire of Scotland/BBC Symphony Orchestra).

www.robbiegordon.org

Jack Nurse – Project Lead and Playwright

Jack is a director and theatre-maker from Dumfries and Galloway and is co-founder of Wonder Fools.

Training: Royal Conservatoire of Scotland and the National Theatre Studio Directors' Course.

As Director: *549: Scots of the Spanish Civil War*, *Home Made*, *McNeill of Tranent*, *The Coolidge Effect* (Wonder Fools); *Larchview* (National Theatre of Scotland); *The Lost Elves*

(Citizens Theatre/Royal Conservatoire of Scotland); *Lampedusa* (Citizens Theatre); *The Mack* (Play, Pie, Pint/ Traverse Theatre).

As Associate/Resident Director: *Red Dust Road* (National Theatre of Scotland/HOME); *The Broons* (Sell A Door); *Dr Dolittle* (Music & Lyrics).

As Assistant Director: *Oresteia: This Restless House* (Citizens Theatre/National Theatre of Scotland); *Blackbird* (Citizens Theatre); *The Winter's Tale* (Royal Lyceum); *Hay Fever* (Royal Lyceum/Citizens Theatre).

www.jacknurse.com

Steph Connell – Producer

Steph has produced for Wonder Fools since 2018 having produced *Stories to Connect Us, 549: Scots of the Spanish Civil War* and *Lampedusa*. She is also Producer of ThickSkin, credits include *Petrichor*, *How Not To Drown*, *AWOL*, *Chalk Farm* and as Assistant Producer for *The Static*. Steph was Stage One Producer at the Citizens Theatre in 2017. Other producing credits include *No Way Back* (Frantic Assembly); Leaper – *A Fish Tale* and *Finding Victoria* (Tucked In); *Full Stop*, *Playground Victories* (Light The Fuse/Scribbled Thought) and *Superhero Snail Boy* (Scribbled Thought). Steph has also worked for Artichoke, National Theatre of Scotland, Greenwich and Docklands International Festival, National Centre for Circus Arts and is currently Project Coordinator at the Tron Theatre.

www.stephconnell.co.uk

Gemma Nicol – Participation Associate

Gemma is co-Artistic Director of Dundee-based theatre company **hidden route** who work with young people and partners from Scotland and beyond to create bold work in unexpected places driven by curiosity and collaboration. She is also a Performing Arts Lecturer at Dundee and Angus College.

After graduating from London's Royal Central School of Speech and Drama, she went on to work as Education Officer in Scotland's largest theatre-based Creative Learning department at Dundee Rep Theatre. As a freelance director, producer and facilitator she worked with organisations including: National Theatre of Scotland; Traverse Theatre; Imaginate; Youth Theatre Arts Scotland; Macrobert and Edinburgh's Festival Theatre. Gemma returned to Dundee Rep in 2012 where she became Head of Rep Engage. Here, she managed, directed and delivered on a diverse range of productions and projects with partners ranging from local community groups to national producing theatres such as York Theatre Royal, Theatre Royal Plymouth, Leeds Playhouse and the RSC.

Lisa Williamson – Participation Associate

Lisa is co-Artistic Director of Dundee-based theatre company **hidden route**.

With a degree in Contemporary Theatre and Performance, Lisa has lead, devised and directed numerous youth theatre productions including original devised performances, site specific theatre and pieces of new writing. Lisa has experience co-ordinating and producing national youth theatre festivals, drama conferences and developing partnerships with organisations including Scottish Youth Theatre, Derby Theatre and Theatre Royal Plymouth.

Lisa was Learning and Engagement Manager at Youth Theatre Arts Scotland where amongst other projects she developed and designed professional development opportunities for youth theatre leaders across the country. Prior to this she was Participation and Young Artists Associate at Dundee Rep Theatre's renowned Engage department where she focused on developing partnerships

and projects to nurture young artists in the North East of
Scotland.

Eilidh Nurse – Assistant Producer

Eilidh graduated from the University of Stirling in 2018 with
a First Class Joint BA Hons in English Literature and Film/
Media. She has worked with organisations and festivals such
as the Wigtown Book Festival, the National Youth Theatre,
the National Student Drama Festival, the Hay Festival, the
CatStrand Arts Centre and the Ayr Gaiety Theatre. Before
joining the Wonder Fools team she was Assistant Producer at
the Watermill Theatre, Newbury, and worked closely with
the Artistic Director on programming and producing their
variety of shows.

As a playwright, Eilidh has been a member of the Traverse
Theatre Young Writers Group and the HighTide
Playwright's Academy. She was a finalist for the 2018
Masterclass Pitch Your Play Competition at Theatre Royal
Haymarket and in early 2019 was mentored by award-
winning playwright Frances Poet after being selected as a
Wigtown Book Festival Regional Writer's Awardee. In
September 2019, she was one of three winners of the Rose
Theatre Kingston's New Writing Festival and received a
rehearsed reading at the Rose with a cast of professional
actors, directed by Fay Lomas. Since then she has been
longlisted for EMERGE 2020 (Flux Theatre/Arcola),
shortlisted for Catalyst 2020 (North Wall, Oxford), longlisted
for Pint-Sized 2020 (Bunker) and was ranked in the top 10
per cent out of 1,500 submissions for the 2020 Verity
Bargate Award (Soho Theatre). Eilidh was recently
longlisted for the inaugural Women's Prize for Playwriting
(Paines Plough/Ellie Keel Productions), making the final
seventy out of 1,169 submissions.

PLAYWRIGHTS

Bea Webster

Bea trained at the Royal Conservatoire of Scotland (BA performance in British Sign Language and English)

Recent writing credits include *Staging Our Futures Project* (Little Cog Theatre); *Squeezy Yoghurt* (National Theatre of Scotland's Scenes for Survival).

Bea's poem, *Long Lost Lover*, about Thailand, her birthplace, was published in both BSL and English. She also wrote and performed in the BBC Social's *How Not To Be D*cks To Deaf People'*. She is one of the Playwright Studio Scotland's mentored playwrights for 2020.

She was nominated Best Actress in a Play at The Stage Debut Awards 2019 for her role of Kattrin in *Mother Courage*. Theatre credits include *The Winter's Tale* (Royal Shakespeare Company)*; Peeling* (Taking Flight Theatre Company); *Mother Courage and Her Children* (Red Ladder Theatre Company).

Chris Thorpe

Chris is a writer and performer from Manchester. He is currently working with China Plate touring his solo piece *Status* internationally and developing the final show in his trilogy in collaboration with Rachel Chavkin. He is Associate Artist at the Royal Exchange, Manchester – work for them includes *There Has Possibly Been An Incident* and *The Mysteries,* and work with their community projects and Young Company. Other theatre work includes *Victory Condition* and *The Milk of Human Kindness* for the Royal Court, as well as an upcoming Royal Court/Methuen commission focusing on the climate crisis and the Royal Court/FT film *What Do You Want Me To Say?* and several shows for the Unicorn Theatre including a new version of *Beowulf*.

He has ongoing collaborations with Rachel Chavkin (*Confirmation/Status/A Family Business*), Lucy Ellinson (TORYCORE), Portugal's mala voadora (*Overdrama/House-Garden/Dead End/Your Best Guess*, and in development *Dying* for the National Theatre of Portugal), Hannah Jane Walker (*The Oh Fuck Moment/I Wish I Was Lonely*) and Rachel Bagshaw, writing *The Shape of the Pain* in 2017 and adapting it for the BBC's Culture in Quarantine in 2020. Chris was a founder member of Unlimited Theatre and is an Associate of live art/theatre company Third Angel with whom he co-wrote and toured *Presumption* and *What I Heard About The World* globally. Other regular collaborators include Yusra Warsama, Javaad Alipoor and Nassim Soleimanpour. Recent work also includes *We Are The King Of Ventilators* directed by Tim Etchells and performed by Jim Fletcher for the Onassis Foundation New York. He is currently working with Melanie Wilson on her upcoming *Artificial Intelligence Project* for Fuel Theatre.

Chris's work tours internationally and is also regularly produced for stage and radio throughout Europe and in the US, including *Victory Condition* at Residenzteater Munich, and the Italian productions of *There Has Possibly Been an Incident* and *Confirmation* were awarded the Premio Franco Enriquez 2018. His work has won multiple Fringe First awards. Chris was the Arvon mentor for playwriting, 2016/17 and works with the National Student Drama Festival.

Stef Smith

Stef Smith is a multi award-winning writer working to international acclaim.

Work includes *Enough, Girl In The Machine, Swallow* (Traverse Theatre); *Nora: A Doll's House* (Glasgow Citizen's Theatre); *The Song Project, Human Animals* (Royal Court); *Acts Of Resistance* (Headlong/Bristol Old Vic); *Love Letter To Europe* (Underbelly); *How To Build A Nation* (Young

Vic); *Remote* (National Theatre Connections Festival); *Tea And Symmetry* (BBC Radio); *Smoke (And Mirrors)* (Traverse Theatre & Dot Istanbul for Theatre Uncut); *Back To Back To Back* (Cardboard Citizens); *Cured* (Glasgay! Festival); *Grey Matter* (The Lemon Tree, Aberdeen); *Woman Of The Year* (Oran Mor, Glasgow) and *Falling/Flying* (Tron, Glasgow).

Stef has won three Scotsman Fringe First Awards for *Roadkill*, *Swallow* and *Enough*. *Roadkill* also won an Olivier Award for Outstanding Achievement in an Affiliate Theatre, a Herald Angel Award, the Amnesty Freedom of Expression Award, a Total Theatre Award for Innovation, and the Edinburgh International Festival Fringe Prize. *Swallow* opened to widespread critical acclaim, and also won the Scottish Arts Club Theatre Award. *Girl in the Machine* won the 2019 Science and Theatre Drama Award in Germany.

Recently Stef took part in the BBC Drama Writersroom and her Digital Drama Short pilot *FLOAT* was released on BBC iPlayer in October 2019.

Stef is currently under commission to the Lyceum Theatre, Guildhall School of Music and Drama, Leeds Playhouse, National Theatre of Scotland, Royal Exchange Theatre and is on attachment at the National Theatre Studio. She is also an Associate Artist at the Traverse Theatre, Leeds Playhouse and Playwrights' Studio, Scotland.

Sabrina Mahfouz

Sabrina's most recent project was her cross-genre show *A History of Water in the Middle East* at the Royal Court Theatre, which she wrote and performed. She is one of the inaugural writers in residence at Shakespeare's Globe Theatre for 2019–20, and is working on theatre and TV projects with the Jermyn Street Theatre, Little Dot Studios and FX. She had three new anthologies published in October 2019 – *Smashing It: Working Class Artists on Life, Art and Making It Happen* (Westbourne Press), which was shortlisted for the

2020 People's Book Prize; *Poems for a Green and Blue Planet* (Hachette Children's) and *Sabrina Mahfouz: Plays 1* (Methuen Drama).

Her theatre work includes *Chef*, a play about an inmate of a women's prison who is also a haute cuisine chef, which won a Fringe First Award; *Dry Ice*, her first play based on her time working in strip clubs, directed by David Schwimmer and for which she was nominated as Best Solo Performer in The Stage Awards for Acting Excellence; *Clean*, a play about three women who work in the criminal underworld, which won a Herald Angel Award and transferred to Off-Broadway in 2015; and *With a Little Bit of Luck*, a gig theatre piece for Paines Plough with a live UK Garage score, which has been performed across the UK, including at the National Theatre and the Roundhouse, and was adapted for BBC 1Xtra radio, where it won the 2019 BBC Music & Radio Award for Best Drama.

Sabrina is the editor of the critically acclaimed anthology *The Things I Would Tell You: British Muslim Women Write* (Saqi Books), a Guardian Book of the Year, and is an essay contributor to the multi-award-winning *The Good Immigrant* (Unbound), exploring her mixed heritage through the lens of British fashion. She won the 2018 King's Arts & Culture Alumni Award for inspiring change in the creative industries.

The Handbook
by Wonder Fools

This handbook was produced to go alongside the Positive Stories for Negative Times participatory project 26 August 2020 — 31 March 2021 to help participating groups to explore, rehearse and record their chosen play. If you're reading this before March 2021 then it tells you how to take part in the project so we'd love you to sign up if you'd like to perform any of the plays. If you're reading this after March 2021, then it contains lots of tips on how to make work remotely or in the space and exercises to help groups to explore each play that can be used at anytime. Enjoy!

Steps of the process

Positive Stories for Negative Times was only dreamt up in April 2020. It has been an incredible experience pulling this together and what we want to say at this point is that due to the project's digital nature we have constantly had to learn as we go, so nothing in this handbook is set in stone. If you want to share some of your own practice or have any suggestions or ideas on how the project can best serve young people please get in touch, we would love to hear from you. We hope you enjoy this process as much as we've loved creating it. It has been an extreme privilege and an adventure in a truly bizarre time.

To help you lead Positive Stories for Negative Times we have created this ten-step process so that the work can happen effectively, safely and creatively.

1. Pick your play
2. Prepare for the process
3. Create a safe space
4. Form positive relationships
5. Foster a creative environment
6. Cast the play
7. Rehearse the play
8. Film the play
9. Upload the play
10. Share the work

If you're reading this before March 2021 and would like to sign up for free, head over to www.positivestories.scot. And if you're reading this after, then please head over to the website anyway to see what we are up to.

1. Pick your play

There are five brilliant plays to choose from at the beginning of the Positive Stories for Negative Times process. All were commissioned after lockdown in March 2020 and so every play responds to the extraordinary experiences and emotions we all went through during that time. In addition, because they were all written during the pandemic all of the plays are able to be performed either in real life or remotely, depending on the context your group is working in and the most recent government guidelines. Here is a little about each play...

Bad Bored Women of the Rooms
by Sabrina Mahfouz

A storytelling adventure through the centuries of women and girls who have spent a lot of time stuck in a room.

Age: 18+
Cast size: can be adapted for one performer to a max of around 20.

The Pack
by Stef Smith

A playful and poetic exploration about getting lost in the loneliness of your living room and trying to find your way home.

Age: 13+
Cast size: Two or two hundred, and everything in-between.

Hold Out Your Hand
by Chris Thorpe

A dynamic text that questions where we are now and the moment we are living through.

Age: 13+
Cast size: 1 – 100

Is This A Fairytale?
by Bea Webster

A fairytale turned inside out in a surprising, inventive and unconventional way. Think damsel in distress, dragons, distinguished knights and depression.

Age: 8+
Cast size: 9 – 20

Ozymandias
by Jack Nurse
& Robbie Gordon

A contemporary story inspired by Percy Shelley's 19th century poem of the same name. A group of ordinary young people hatch a daring plan to do something extraordinary.

Age 16+
Cast size: 1 – 100

2. Prepare your process

Introduction

In all likelihood, most of you will have led creative processes live in the space, so preparing this one might feel a little different if it's going to happen online. Some of you may have never led a creative process before and that's totally fine, that's what this handbook is for.

Wonder Fools have been extremely lucky since the pandemic hit. From the comfort of our own living rooms, we've been up and down the country chatting to organisations online about thoughts, concerns and questions ahead of a new term and academic year that will be wildly different from anything that has come before.

Some people have said:

> *"We are excited about the year ahead, but we are concerned about safety."*

Others have said:

> *"This is uncharted territory and I hope my practice transfers to the online space so that my group can continue effectively."*

And some have simply said:

> *"AAAAAGGGGHHHH!"*

We are here to help and share practice through this handbook, which is the culmination of conversations, trying things out and stealing. Yes, stealing. Or should we call it borrowing. Yes, we will call it borrowing. We are fervent believers that creative practice is all about looking at what's out there and cherry-picking exercises, ideas and strategies that suit your group, your style and whatever particular context that you work in.

Our beliefs

There are a few things that you will need in place before you start this process – whether that's physically or digitally. When Wonder Fools are preparing projects we think firstly about creating a safe environment for young people and to do so we embed the same principles into all of the work that we make.

There are three cornerstones of any Wonder Fools participatory work:

1. Create an open, safe and inclusive space.
2. Engender positive relationships through active listening, storytelling and discussion.
3. Foster a creative and fun environment to work in.

In tandem with our principles about creating and making participatory work we have firmly held organisational beliefs about safeguarding the children, young people and vulnerable adults that we work with:

- The welfare and safety of children and young people should always be protected and promoted.
- Children and young people are individuals with their own needs, wishes and feelings.
- Children and young people should be able to use the internet for education and personal development, but safeguards need to be in place to ensure they are always kept safe.

It's best to think about your personal and organisational principles and how to best achieve them in a digital space. You may already have your own set of beliefs or values and if you do that's brilliant. If you don't that's absolutely fine too. This project is potentially a catalyst to create them, redefine them or make them futureproof.

What you will need

Importantly, as well as a set of beliefs and values you will need the following in place in order to begin work online:

- Child Protection Policy
- Designated Child Protection Officer
- Criminal record checks in place
- Online Code of Conduct for staff
- Online Code of Conduct for young people
- Child protection training
- Preventative measures and response to bullying and online abuse
- Risk assessment
- Permission slips

Technology

We use six low-cost pieces of software that enable us to lead our participatory work online. We are not tied to everyone using the same software but we wanted to share a wee bit about what we've been using.

The six pieces of software we've been working with are:

1. Zoom for online classes, workshops and rehearsals.
2. WeTransfer for the transfer of large video files.
3. Dropbox for the secure storage of files.
4. FinalCut Pro for the editing of videos.
5. YouTube for the sharing of work (both publicly and privately).
6. Eventbrite for creating a public facing event for your final performance.

1. ZOOM
We lead our classes on Zoom. This is where we meet our groups, lead exercises and set tasks. At the time of writing, the Pro account is £11.99 a month with no time limit and free cloud storage for recording meetings. If you are a charity, you can receive half price membership through Charity Digital Exchange. We think Zoom is the best software for online teaching having experimented with Microsoft Teams, Google Hangouts and Webex. There are multiple reasons for this including cost, accessibility, additional features and the 'democracy' of the space. Although, you should always check if the security and privacy features are right for your organisation.

2. WE TRANSFER
When we set tasks on Zoom we often ask for the submission to be in the form of short videos. We want the young people we work with to get into the practice of creating high quality video content and learning the basics of this ahead of the creation of the final performance. Wonder Fools finds WeTransfer the most effective way of transferring large video files from participants to the company. It is easy to use and gives young people a simple and streamlined way to get their work to us. WeTransfer's free limit upload is 2GB which we have never found to be a problem when using it during a process like this one.

3. DROPBOX
We use Dropbox for the secure storage of any video files so when young people send their weekly video submissions, we keep them somewhere safe until we approach the final edit of the work. Your organisation will also likely have cloud storage in place such as Sharepoint or Google Drive, if not this is an easy to use and cheap piece of software that you could use for this project and beyond.

4. FINAL CUT PRO
Our process thus far has consisted of inviting young people to film from their homes and giving them the opportunity to learn to create a more filmic style of work. This process has meant that we as a company have needed to edit the videos together once they are submitted to create the final show. We use Final Cut Pro, which is currently available (at the time of writing) for a 90 day free trial. This will give you professional quality editing software to use during the pandemic. We have been so impressed with its ability to add production value to our work and its relatively easy-

to-use interface that we have now purchased the full product. We would recommend Final Cut Pro as a free but high quality editing software with lots of tutorials online to get you started. Although there are also many options if you're looking for editing software including: Adobe Premiere Pro, Lightworks and Davinci Resolve.

If you are asking young people to do some of their own editing there are a number of free apps available including: Splice, Adobe Premiere Clip, Quik and iMovie.

5. YOUTUBE

We have found YouTube to be the best platform to share our work – both privately and publicly. YouTube is free to use and the different privacy settings are: public (everyone can see it), private (you and anyone you choose can see it) and unlisted (can be seen and shared by anyone with the link). We use YouTube during workshops to upload an edited-together version of the different material generated during a task, set to private, which allows everyone to see all the work of the group without having to download huge video files. For public facing work, we've found that using YouTube's premiere function – which you may have seen used by National Theatre Live amongst others – generates an excitement for participants, subscribers and audiences with a shareable watch page and a countdown clock that adds to the feeling of it being a live event. For this project, we will share all final work using YouTube and host the videos on www.positivestories.scot for each company, creating an event around each individual production.

6. EVENTBRITE

For every public facing outcome of the digital processes we have undertaken, we have used Eventbrite to create a focus and a buzz around the final performance and we encourage you to do the same. Eventbrite allows you to create a listing for an event – we think of it as serving the same function as a box office might in a theatre. It does all the same things: creates a page for your event with all the information and provides a ticketing service. We have found that the simple act of creating an event around groups' final performances has enabled us to enlarge our audience engagement, increase our capacity for fundraising through donations and create an excitement around the event that makes young people feel something similar to how they might feel if their show was on in a theatre. It's important that you don't charge for the work during this project but you can create a donation ask for anyone tuning in to the show to raise money for the important continuation of future activities.

3. Create a safe space

To provide a platform for creativity and meaningful discussion, participants first have to know they are working in a group that is open, safe and inclusive.

You might want to do one, two, or all of these following exercises and strategies or invent your own way of creating a safe space. This section of the pack is to further support your safeguarding work and the young people in the group and to create a positive environment for working on the plays. You may have your own strategies and we would love to hear about them but here are a few we've used or heard about whilst running our digital safeguarding sessions back in July 2020.

Check In

Aims:
- To provide an opportunity for participants to voice anything they are feeling, thinking or questioning on any given day.
- Establish a safe space.
- Allow every individual to feel heard.

Instructions:
A check in is a moment at the beginning of a session where group leaders and participants can hear from everyone in the room about how they are feeling. It is useful for the beginning of a process or workshops and can establish a regular way of the group connecting with one another. This exercise also allows participants to begin to practicae active listening which will be the bedrock for any discussion and group work.

1. Say to the group that you are going to "Check In".
2. Ask each individual member how they are today.
3. Encourage the rest of the group to listen and wait until it is their turn to speak.
4. Listen intently and respond accordingly, ensuring that every participant feels heard and connected.

Technology:
Depending on the group, you might want to encourage every participant to mute themselves until it is their turn to speak to enable a more focussed space.

Adaptations & Advancements:
You can really play around with how you frame check in depending on the group you are working with for example:

- Check in with one word.
- Check in by saying what colour you feel like today.
- Check in by saying what animal you feel like today (or any other similar variation).
- Check in with a thematic question linked to the enquiry of the piece.

You can also lead a check out, either as a held discussion as described or through any of the adaptations. This can allow you to assess how the session has gone for individual participants, for example: someone might reveal a more positive outlook than at the beginning because of the workshop or someone might discuss a negative reaction to a part of the workshop that you hadn't picked up on. This might be a great strategy for also logging the impact of your sessions for evaluation purposes.

Group Charter

Aims:
To draw up a list of principles about how the group will work together.

Instructions:
This is an exercise that allows groups to get on the same page – literally! Your charter will be a document listing shared principles that form a collective understanding of how the group will work together.

1. Establish the aims of the exercise, as stated above.
2. Ask everyone to make a list that begins "I would like this group to..." and spend around two minutes writing answers focussing on positives.
   - Examples include "I would like this group to be respectful"; "I would like this group to listen carefully to what everyone has to say"; and "I would like this group to always try their best".
3. Ask each individual to share their list back to the group.
4. Write a list of shared principles based on the individual lists of the young people.
5. Agree as a group to sign up to these principles and agree to work in this way moving forward.

Technology:
Utilise the "share screen" function on Zoom so participants can see the charter as you write it.

Adaptations & Advancements:
You can also frame this as a contract and ask everyone to add their name onto a Google Doc at the end of the document. This signing off can, dependent on the group and context, allow for a stronger sense of enlisting to what has been written.

Safe Space Drop-ins

Aims:
To ensure young people are safe and that they have a space to report anything that they are worried about.

Instructions:
This is a strategy that could be deployed if you are working with a group fully online. When working with groups earlier on in the pandemic we were concerned that the typical ways of recognising when young people were at harm would be much more difficult online particularly in relation to the NSPCC guidelines on recognising the signs of abuse. Therefore, we had to come up with a system that gave a safe space to young people within our online sessions similar to what would be traditionally available in the room.

1. Set up times before and after sessions where young people can talk about how they feel outside of the creative process.

2. In the 'before' sessions it should be a group discussion such as a check in where everyone can share a bit about how they are doing and if they have any thoughts, questions or concerns as a result of the pandemic and/or otherwise.
   • This space was particularly useful in the wake of exam results.
3. At the end of the 'before' part of the session, let everyone know that there will be an additional private space at the end of the session for anyone that has any thoughts, questions or concerns that they are unable to share with the wider group or want to speak about further with the staff.
4. The session runs as normal and at the end the facilitators re-assert if anyone wants to stay to talk about anything then the space will stay open.
5. In the 'after' part of the session, if any young people stay behind you can talk to them about any problems or issues they may have in an online private space.
6. Make sure you are not on your own and that you are working with someone else in this context. Over the last few months we have partnered with a youth worker who added value and knowledge to these spaces. If anything is disclosed to you that suggests a child is at risk or harm follow policies to make sure that the child or young person is protected.

Technology:
If multiple people stay behind you can schedule times for them to click back onto the Zoom link for a conversation. Make sure you have enabled the waiting room function so that young people can enter whenever the facilitators are ready to speak to them and so that young people cannot re-enter without being admitted, ensuring the privacy of the space.

Adaptations & Advancements:
When we worked with organisations across Scotland on the child protection training aspect of this project we spoke to one organisation in particular who were using a similar way of working. They talked to all of the participants on an individual basis on the day of their classes and also used a numerical scale to track the wellbeing of their participants throughout the project. This meant the facilitator could objectively view and chart young people's wellbeing and follow up if needed. This could be incredibly useful if you are working with at-risk young people.

Online Tips and Tricks

Now, let's talk about Zoom. It might be hard to create a safe space when you don't have full control over the room but we've got a few things that you can do to make the space more comfortable and democratic:

• Encourage participants and staff to place themselves on mute when they are not speaking.
• Encourage participants to use gallery view to see everyone at the same time.
• Read out the Code of Conduct for any new participants. This restating of the rules and values of the group will embed an awareness of how young people should behave and help reduce the risk of any safeguarding issues.
• Create a step-by-step guide to show how to get onto Zoom for the participants and their families.

These are a selection of potential strategies and methods for creating a safe space and it's up to you and the young people to define the system that works best for your organisation.

4. Form positive relationships

Allows group participants to galvanise as a group, form meaningful relationships and become a collective sounding board for each other.

Once you have begun to run a safe space it's important that you now start to develop connections within the group and begin to build an ensemble; this is much more difficult if you're approaching this work online. But not impossible. We aim to create an environment which encourages active listening and champions empathy whether we're in the room or online. We've created a few examples of work we've used online that will hopefully begin to get young people working together collaboratively and communicating effectively. All of these exercises can also be led in the room.

The Big Unanswerable Question

Aims:
To get the group on the same page, collectively interrogating the themes of the work, and to set an enquiry to regularly return to throughout the project.

Instructions:
We always like to come up with a big unanswerable question when starting our projects. A question that we can return to throughout the project to frame discussion and track our developing understanding of the work we are making.

For 549: Scots of the Spanish Civil War, a play about the rise of the right wing presently and historically, we asked "Can we truly learn from our history?" in response to a George Wilhelm Fredrich Hegel quote. For The Coolidge Effect, a play about heavy internet and pornography usage, we asked: "How does pornography affect our mental health, relationships and sexual experiences?". And for Lampedusa, our staging of Anders Lustgarten's play about the migrant crisis we asked: "How can we understand someone else's lived experience from a position of relative privilege?". For this project, just like all of the others, we will define an enquiry question that will underpin the process and making of the work. Especially when we are devising or working on short timelines everything we do in the room should refer back to the enquiry we have set, helping us to keep on task but also make cohesive and interrogative shows.

1. Explain the concept of the big unanswerable question and its purpose. It should be a question that you do not know the answer to but something that you'd like to gain a deeper understanding of as a result of the project.
   - If you are working on Stef Smith's play an example enquiry could be: "Why do we all feel loneliness at some point in our lives?"
   - If you are working on Chris Thorpe's play an example enquiry could be: "What can we take from this pandemic as we dream of the future?"
   - If you are working on Sabrina Mahfouz's play an example enquiry could be: "Why are the females of our history not treated the same as men?"
   - If you are working on Wonder Fools' play an example enquiry could be: "What is the significance of tearing down statues and what change can it create?"
   - If you are working on Bea Websters' play an example enquiry could be:

"Why do we demonise those who are different from us?" or even "Why are princesses always women in fairy tales?"

2. Tell the group they have a few minutes to write every single question that they can think of that could form a good 'Big Unanswerable Question'.

3. Put on a track of ambient music that is around a few minutes in length, preferably with no lyrics (our favourites tracks for exercises like these are by Four Tet, Bonobo or Aphex Twin).

4. When the few minutes are up get everyone to choose their favourite question and explain that this is a question they can personally return to throughout the process. It might also be good if you as the facilitator can keep a log of these as they may serve the purpose of creating a really nice reflection point towards the end of the process to see what the individual has learned as a result of making the show.

5. Get everyone to share their questions one by one and work with the group to find an enquiry question that most fits the group's shared interests. This could be a long discussion process that allows for people to talk about ideas and where they are coming from in relation to the play and is fantastic groundwork for getting into the rehearsal process. You might settle on one or create a new one based on a combination of ideas (see the above example of The Coolidge Effect enquiry question, which names the three most central ideas of the play).

6. At the end of this task you will have a collective enquiry question for the group and every participant will have an individual one.

Technology:

If you're using Zoom and on step three (above) when playing the track of music you can either utilise the screen share function, which has a tick box for sharing sound, or pop the link to the track in the chat box so they can listen to it on their device. Get everyone to pop themselves on mute for this bit to make sure the track comes through clearly and there's no feedback.

Adaptations & Advancements:

If you are in real space you could work with getting all of the young people to write their personal enquiry down on a sheet of A4 and place them across the room. Lead an exercise that gets one person at a time to change the placing of pieces of paper around the space. The idea is that the enquiry that resonates most strongly with them should sit in the centre of the room and they are not allowed to choose their own enquiry. The young people can take this in turns and actively watch each other and see what ideas regularly land in the middle. This is a great exercise for seeing how subjective ideas and thoughts are and also means that the young people can have a nuanced discussion at the end of the exercise about the enquiries that resonated with people the most. This exercise is both democratic and performative, it allows people to vote with their feet as opposed to the person with the loudest voice or most to say dominating the conversation.

Treasure Hunt

Aims:
To get the ensemble telling stories, learning about each other and also finding the creative opportunities in working from home.

Instructions:
Frame this task as a storytelling exercise.

1. Tell the group that they need to find something in their home based on a theme and that they are going to tell a story about it.
2. Tell them that the best story gets a point and the best object gets a point. These will be "drama points" and totally arbitrary but we always find a bit of excitement and focus is generated if the group thinks it's a competition.
3. Choose the theme and count down from three. Give them a minute.
   The theme could be:
   - The oldest thing you could find.
   - An object that holds the most value.
   - An object that is blue.
   - An object beginning with the letter "W".
4. Watch your group run around frantically trying to find an object and come up with a story.
5. Hear the stories and give the points out to the people with the best objects and stories.
   - We've had all sorts that young people have come back with: dogs, 100 year old clocks and even grannies.

Technology:
Encourage the young people to stop sharing video whilst they run around trying to find their object as it adds to the suspense and drama of the game.

Adaptations & Advancements:
You can find dramatic links in this game so that it either builds material for productions, creates a nice introduction to themes you will be working with or even helps you find props that young people have in their homes that will be useful in the making of the show.

Would I Lie To You?

Aims:
A wee silly game to get the group telling stories, performing and learning about each other.

Instructions:
Let the groups know this is a game, a bit of fun, but there can only be one winner!

1. Ask the group to grab a pen and paper.
2. Tell them they need to think of two truths and a lie about themselves. They should be little short stories in their own right that they need to prepare to be questioned on. It's worth letting them know that they should find the most

unbelievable truths to make the lie seem more believable. Give the group a few minutes to come up with these and maybe even play a track of music whilst they are thinking.

3. Split the group in half and pit both sides against each other. There will now be a Group A and Group B (or whatever they would like to call themselves?)
4. Ask someone from A to tell their two truths and their lie; and Group B gets to ask them three questions.
5. Ask Group B to vote for which of the three stories they think is a lie and if they are right they get a point.
6. This process is repeated until everyone has had their chance to tell their two truths and a lie and the winning team is announced.

Technology:
If you are working online you could ask the two groups to go into break out rooms on Zoom so that they can confer and help each other rehearse their two truths and a lie. This helps build peer-to-peer feedback mechanisms and also allows them to start thinking about how to help each other tell stories, which might be particularly useful if you are approaching one of the plays that has space for devising.

Adaptations & Advancements:
You can work in small groups so that they find collective truths and lies. For example, "We have all been on the Pepsi Max at Blackpool Pleasure Beach" or "We are all allergic to Vimto". It will allow a bit of a breakout space for the young people to work peer-to-peer and also find common ground without the conversation being facilitated by the group leader.

5. Foster a creative environment

Allows participants the freedom to be creative and artistic by delivering initial exercises that indicate the process will be fun and engaging.

These are exercises to get your group kickstarted back into being creative. A lot of them are about the young people having fun, performing and making theatre again! They are great for the start of creative processes and individual workshops online and in real space.

Continuous Writing

Aims:
To get the young people exploring themes, characters and thoughts through creative writing.

Instructions:
Many people use creative writing in a multitude of ways but we have been finding it an incredibly effective method to get young people working with text and performing on Zoom. It's quick, easy and active. If it's framed correctly it can also lead to the creation of interesting material and allow young people to explore parts of the play they might not have thought about otherwise.

1. Find an aspect of the play you want to focus on and explore.
2. Now find a refrain. This is a repeated phrase that will form the basis of your continuous writing task. It will be the opening line of the text and also the line that the young people can return to if they get stuck. Explain to the young people that whenever they get stuck they should just keep writing this phrase again and again until a new thought forms. Here examples based on a few of the plays:
   - If you are exploring Sabrina's the refrain might be "I am a bad bored woman in a room."
   - If you are exploring Bea's the refrain might be "princesses are..."
   - If you are exploring Chris' you might alternate between two refrains: "Something to keep..." and "Something to let go of..."
3. Ask the group to grab a pen and paper. Explain to them that they have to write continuously without stopping for the length of a song. Pick a track, preferably with no lyrics and play.
4. At the end of the track give the young people time and space to edit their writing. Encourage them to take out anything that they don't feel is relevant or anything that they don't feel comfortable sharing. Writing continuously can be an emotional experience for some young people so really give them a bit of time to read their writing back and decide what they want to share.
5. Set up a sharing of the work with everyone taking it in turns to read and reflect on what this exercise has taught the group about the play or even themselves in relation to the play.

Technology:
If you are working on Zoom you can utilise the share audio function for the sharing and you can play the song that they've been listening to to write their text as an

underscore. This works particularly well if the tracks have no lyrics and it also gives a heightened sense of performance to the sharing of their work.

Adaptations & Advancements:
You can get the young people to pop themselves on mute and give them a good bit of time to rehearse the text. Where could it take place within their home? Can you challenge them to use props? Could they trade texts with someone else in the group? This could actually create additional content for them to show their families or you could use to post on social media to generate interest from audiences ahead of the show.

5 Words — Movement Exercise

Aims:
To get the young people moving about, using their bodies to explore the ideas in the play and generating material that can be used in the final performances.

Instructions:
When thinking about making movement online compared to in the theatre we were initially quite anxious. It was uncharted territory. There was less safe space to explore and also the conditions vary from house to house. What we wanted to do was lean into the space that young people had or didn't have as part of the exploration. We really wanted to encourage movement that adapts to the environment and context. But also, really importantly, we wanted to get young people up and moving out of their chairs. This is a really simple movement exercise that will get this process started and most other movement exercises can be adapted to play by these rules.

1. Pick a page of text, one that might benefit from the inclusion of adding movement or even one that just has rich ideas that you would like to explore physically.
2. Ask the group to find 5 words on that page, which have the most meaning to them. The 5 most exciting and important words.
3. Ask the young people to clear a space in the room that they are in of any trip hazards and anything that they might bump into. Within that space ask them now to walk in a circle. No matter how big or small that circle is. Get them to really understand the space that they have at their disposal. And then ask them to centre themselves in the middle of that circle.
4. Ask the group to create 5 movements, one for each word they have chosen, that use the space in their circle. Any movement they make shouldn't leave that circle and should always return to the centre.
5. Once they have the five movements they should create a sequence that ties the movements together and loops.
6. Once they have finished making their sequence encourage the group to share their sequences one by one.
7. Reflect on the exercise and frame a question to the group.
   - Is it something you could incorporate into the final production?
   - Has anyone gained a deeper understanding of the text?
   - Has anyone learned anything about their character?

Technology:
For the sharing you can define an order of participants in the chat box as a list
of names and share audio to play a track. This means there will be a free-flowing
sharing of the work that young people can watch, participate in and enjoy.

Adaptations & Advancements:
You can pick the best movements from each member of the group's sequences and
string them together to create an ensemble movement piece that everyone can
perform in unison.

Create A Trailer

Aims:
To get the young people making material, having fun and beginning to articulate
what the show they're working on is about.

Instructions:
This is a bit of silly fun particularly for younger groups but also totally appropriate
for older groups to explore their silly side too. It's all about being able to talk about
the themes of the piece and begin to further understand the process they are
involved in.

1. Show an over the top Hollywood trailer. Look at ones by Don LaFontaine. There
   are some really good compilations of his trailers online. He says things like "IN
   A WORLD, WHERE NOTHING MEANS ANYTHING ANYMORE, TWO COPS,
   WILL SAVE A DOG" in an overly dramatic and epic voice. Ok, we made that one
   up but you get the drift. Google him.
2. Use a trailer like this one as your stimulus. One that's super over the top and aim
   to create your own version.
3. First of all, get the young people to think about the play they're working on: eke
   out the story beats, find the characters and create their own cliff-hanger that will
   hook people in to watch. Even if it's something that you will never film or show.
4. You might split into groups to rehearse this or work as one big company.
5. Share the "trailer" back and reflect on what the group has learned as a result of
   the exercise.

Technology:
You could rehearse and share this back like you would share a scene in the room or
you could go one step further and fully film and edit it. You could do this by asking
the young people to film individual lines of the text you make and send them back to
you. You would then simply edit it together and find some epic rights-free music to
underscore. Look into YouTube's Audio Library for rights-free music. This might
also give you a chance as the facilitator to get to grips with any editing software
you might use ahead of making the final performance.

Adaptations & Advancements:
You could find other forms of trailers to parody or mimic. For example, you could
explore a cinematic style that just has images of actions, key lines and a dramatic
score. It's totally up to you. The idea at the end of the exercise is that young people
will be able to talk about the work they are doing and what it means.

6. Cast the play

All five plays are scalable in terms of how many young people can be involved. We want to help every group to be able to stage their play – if you think your group is too large for a given play and would like ideas on how to get everyone involved then read on.

The following are suggestions for casting each play. There will of course be other ways too — have a think about your group and what works best for them individually and collectively.

Bad Bored Women Of The Rooms

Cast size: Can be adapted for between one performer to a max of around 20.

One way of expanding beyond 20 is for a different group of actors (say, between 5–10) to take each individual story and recipe. Perhaps there is a different member of the group that plays each woman we meet throughout history. There could also be non-speaking roles such as roles that could enact the recipes. This is an especially good strategy if there are young people in your group who want to be in the show but might not want a speaking part.

The story is all about criminal and mischievous women throughout history but this doesn't mean that it is female only – quite the opposite. How often are there plays dominated by male voices that have to be performed by girls and women because there haven't been parts written for them? Men and boys might learn as a result of this process by stepping aside, sharing space and celebrating female narratives.

The Pack

Cast size: 2 or 200, and everything in-between.

Stef's writing allows as many different people as possible to be involved. There's a scene between two characters threaded throughout and you have the option of two young people playing those specific roles throughout – or not!

Hold Out Your Hand

Cast size: 1 – 100

Similar to The Pack, Chris has written a text that any group of young people of any number can perform.

Is This A Fairytale?

Cast size: 9 – 20

This play has specific characters for young people to perform so think about the different characteristics of your class or group and who is best suited to the different roles. If your class has more than 20 young people, then use the Jester characters to find everyone a line – divide all the Jester lines up between everyone who doesn't have a named part. Maybe there's people in your class that have a single line and three or four jesters that take the bulk of the dialogue, again see what works best for your group of young people. As per Bea's instructions, once the characters are cast you can change the pronouns in the text to suit who is playing each role.

Ozymandias

Cast size: 1 – 100

Any size of group can tackle Ozymandias. The many different voices of the young people will add up to create an exciting chorus of narrators and storytellers. Important note for casting the characters in the piece: Alex is a female person of colour; Joe is a white male and the rest is up to you. Feel free to change Tattie or any of the other supporting characters' gender pronouns depending on your group.

Other Roles

Before you cast the play, have a wee think about other roles young people could have in the creation of the performance. If you teach a classroom or lead a group where there are young people who are less confident in performing, or who simply wish to act in the final performance, then there's a variety of different tasks to choose from. Here is a list of other roles the young people could be fulfil (it's not exhaustive!):

Director   **Stage manager**

Assistant director   **Costume designer**

Set designer

Front of house   **Musician**

Camera operator   **Social media manager**

This process works best when the whole group is involved and they have ownership over the final show. Giving people roles that contribute to the final performance is an excellent strategy for involving those who are hard to reach or engage with. Think School of Rock but theatre!

7. Rehearse the play

Now that you have created a safe space, formed positive relationships and fostered a creative environment it is time to rehearse the play.

We don't want to be too prescriptive in how you rehearse your plays, so we have written down some ideas, provocations and suggestions for each part of the process that you can follow to the letter, completely discard or use as inspiration in how you structure your time in rehearsals. We have deliberately left space for you to follow the process that you'd like to lead and we genuinely can't wait to see the results.

Every rehearsal process we undertake has different layers to it: an initial exploration, then experimentation, followed by familiarisation. This all culminates in the final performance.

Initial Exploration

This part of the process sets the foundations for the work you do on the script. You hear it aloud for the first time, discuss with the group the key ideas and themes and begin to immerse yourself in the world of the play.

At the start of the process, you should have a **readthrough** of the script with all the young people. If we were in the room, we would do this in a circle but Zoom's democracy of space gives a similar feel. If you have already cast the play then get those specific people to read their parts. Alternatively, if the parts or lines aren't allocated yet then determine an order of people to read one different line of dialogue at a time. You can use the chat box on Zoom to write an order that people can refer to, or ask them to use the old-fashioned pen and paper...

The readthrough is an exciting moment at the start of the process but also a potentially nerve-racking one for people having to read out loud in front of their friends or peers for maybe the first time. Be aware of this and observe if anyone seems really withdrawn – they may just need an extra little bit of help and encouragement.

Alongside the readthrough, it's a good idea to give the young people an **overview of the process** – how exactly the next days, weeks, or months are going to work. You will probably have already sent out details of the process beforehand but going through exactly what getting the performance together and filming it will take gets everyone on the same page from the start.

After you've done the readthrough, ask the group what they think and how it makes them feel. Wonder Fools always facilitates a **theme exercise** to underpin the rehearsals at the beginning with a shared understanding of the central ideas in the play we're working on. Whether we are leading a process with young people or professional actors, we always ask the same question: "What is the play about?". The simpler the answers the better, Ozymandias might be about "friendship" or "power", The Pack might be about "loneliness" or "fear", Is This A Fairytale? might be about "rewriting stories" or "mental health", Hold Out Your Hand might be about "dreams" or "connection" and Bad Bored Women of the Rooms might be about "women in history" or "neglected female stories" – draw up a list of answers from the group. This bank of words and phrases are the themes of the play. It's a good time for us to mention a core principle of Wonder Fools' work in the room – there are no bad ideas! Having taken everybody's suggestions you can now read them aloud and consult with the group to see if you can narrow the list down to three or four main themes. These are the central ideas in the play and you can keep referring back to these as rehearsals progress as a shorthand for discussing what the play is about. Tip – in the room we write all the themes on post it notes so we can see them all and online we use a word document and "Share Screen" function on Zoom so that the group have something to look at as they discuss the themes.

Another crucial part of the initial exploration in rehearsals is making sure that everyone understands everything in the text. An additional core principle of Wonder Fools' work is that there are no silly questions! Allow in the early stages of rehearsals a culture of asking questions. How this works depends largely on how you are rehearsing the play and what age group you are working with. This could be as simple as reading the play in sections after the readthrough and at the end asking the group if they have any questions about characters, plot, dialogue, themes OR this could be a natural process as you rehearse scenes/sections up on their feet whereby you encourage the young people to ask questions if something is unclear. The crucial thing is making sure that the young people understand every part of the script because that will make sure they are confident in their performances and in their approach to rehearsing the play.

There have been numerous exercises in Parts 3, 4 and 5 that also allow you to explore the themes and ideas of the different plays. Make sure you have a look through these sections as you plan your rehearsals and embed these exercises into the process of exploring the plays.

Experimentation

This part of the process is all about playing with the source material – finding out who the characters are and/or what each young person is bringing to the text. It is also the place to try out the different exercises that have room for young people's individual responses, if your play includes any.

There are a number of different ways you can approach experimenting with the text which we will leave up to you. Some questions to think about:

- How do the characters or storytellers sound, look and move?
- What are the different ways of showing the story as well as telling it?
- What different rhythms work best for the different sections in the plays with narration?
- If you have the capacity for this, would music work under certain moments?
- What is the most interesting way of starting the performance?
- What is the most interesting way of finishing the performance?

This is the moment in the process where you can try things out and if they don't work that's amazing because you've tested an idea and most likely found out a different way of doing things. This is the moment to explore the individual tasks within certain plays.

Hold Out Your Hand
by Chris Thorpe

Better Titles Exercise

"List all the titles you can come up with that would be better"

Group Exercise:
- Do this after the initial exploration so that everybody has a firm grasp on the play before coming up with your own titles.
- Generate a big list of possible titles without filtering before going back through and choosing as a group the ones you think are better than Chris' efforts... Be honest! The final list is what makes it into the performance.
- If online, use a word document and the share screen function on Zoom to create the list and then go through and highlight the titles you think are better.

Worst Moment Exercise

"The worst moment one of you remembers most clearly about 2020 so far – it can be a different moment from a different person every performance"

Group Exercise:
- Talk to the group about 2020 and put the year into context. Hear about their experiences.
- Ask the group to each write down their worst moment from 2020 on a piece of paper – let them know that this will be heard by the rest of the group and that to approach this exercise with caution. Encouraging them to only share something that they are comfortable with.
- One by one, go around the group and hear from them their worst moments. Let people know that it's also ok to not share if they don't want to. They might have written something that they thought would initially be ok to share but isn't now. Changing minds is fine. It's been an emotional time for everyone.
- Leave space after hearing from everybody to see if anyone has a reflection or response to anything that has been shared from the group.
- Following the exercise, you can choose which worst moment is included in the show – if you are doing more than one performance perhaps this can change from show to show.

Best Moment Exercise

"The best moment one of you remembers most clearly about 2020 so far – it can be a different moment from a different person every performance if you are doing it multiple times."

Group Exercise:
- Talk to the group about 2020 and put the year into context looking at the positives this time. Hear about their experiences.
- Ask the group to each write down their best moment from 2020 on a piece of paper — let them know that this will be heard by the rest of the group.
- One by one, go around the group and hear from them their best moment.
- Leave a moment after hearing from everybody to see if anyone has a reflection or response to anything that has been shared from the group.
- Following the exercise, you can choose which best moment is included in the show — if you are doing more than one performance perhaps this will change from show to show.

What Was It Like?
"What was it like for you?"

Group Exercise:
- Discuss the images in the text (the repeating frame in a montage in a film and the blank bus stop timetable) and hear from the group what they think these mean.
- Ask the group to write three of their own images that evoke the same kind of feeling for them.
- Give them a couple of minutes to complete the task — put a track of music on if you have the capacity to do this.
- At the end of the time, ask them to share back what they think is the strongest image that will resonate the most.
- Hear back from the group, leaving space for any reflections.
- You can either choose the three strongest images to be included in the performance or leave it to the person saying each line to use their own image.

Dream
"One sentence about a dream one of you had in the last few months"

Group Exercise:
- Ask the group to think of a dream they have had of themselves in the last few months.
- Ask them to undertake a continuous writing exercise for five minutes sharing what this dream was like.
- Put a track of music on if you have the capacity to do this.
- Hear back from the group about their experiences of their dreams. This is a space to talk about how peoples' dreams were affected during lockdown and also in a wider sense about dreams and their role in both the play and our lives
- Hear back from the group and talk about any reflections.
- Now ask them to condense their dream into one sentence — how they would sum it up to describe it to another person?
- It is up to you to choose which dreams to include in the final performance.

Glad or Sad to Lose
"Something you were glad to lose, or sad to lose"

Group Exercise:
- Discuss the content for this part of the play — what it would feel like to be in the dream.

Then move on to discussing what parts of the world, of life, young people would be glad to lose or sad to lose.

This can be an open discussion and you can make a list of all the different responses on a piece of paper in the room or if online, use the chat box on Zoom and spend a couple of minutes filling it up as a group with different responses. Discuss with the group which responses resonate with them the most and why? Then find four to include in the show.

A Fountain. There's A...
"There's a (what?)"

Group Exercise:
- Explain the context of the moment to the group.
- Then say you are going to play a game — you will say someone's name and they have to respond with "There's a...." and say whatever comes into their head first — it could be anything, the only rule is it has to be the first thing!
- Play this a few times to ensure the spontaneity of the exercise — once something has been said, it cannot be repeated.
- If you can, and permissions for the group allow, record this so you can look back with the group at all the responses.
- Together, pick three of the best responses to follow "a fountain" and put them in the performance.

Looking Forward
"What do you want in a year from now?"

Group Exercise:
- Ask the group to think about themselves in a year's time and where they see themselves.
- Ask them the question: "what do you want in a year from now?"
- Ask the group to write a short text about where they see themselves in a year's time and what they want.
- Then perform these back to the group.
- Hear from everyone individually and facilitate a discussion around hopes, dreams ad how we can move on from the pandemic.
- Choose three to include in the final performance, adapting the texts to make them shorter if necessary.

Keep or Let Go
"Something to keep. Something to let go of"

Group Exercise:
- Ask the group to write a list of something they'd like to keep.
- Hear back from the group — establish an order and hear from one person at a time and make your way through everyone's lists, finishing when everyone has said everything they have written. It would be lovely to accompany this with a piece of music, if you have the capacity for this.
- Go back through the lists and ask the group to highlight as many as they want to include in the final performance.
- This is your list for the final moment — split the lines up so that the dialogue is alternated between speakers like the rest of the text.
- Repeat for "something they'd like to let go of."

Bad Bored Women of the Rooms
by Sabrina Mahfouz

Lockdown Task
"Add in things the performers have done in their rooms over lockdown that they are genuinely or ironically proud of or are totally mundane but still a success considering our situation – show if appropriate!"

Group Exercise:
- Ask the group to think of three things they were genuinely or ironically proud of or things that are mundane but still a success. Get them to write them down – give them a good few minutes to do this – put a track of music on whilst they do if you can.
- Come back into the circle or the Zoom room and share back everyone's responses.
- After hearing from everyone, reflect on what you've heard from the group.
- Then ask the group to choose one of their three things and spend ten minutes or so finding a way of showing this. If you have a weekly class this could be a homework task or, depending on your process and the type of final performance, you can ask them to make a video of this too.
- You can then choose which responses you'd like to include in the final show.

Ending Celebration Task
"Performers add in here things to celebrate about their lives, futures, hopes – real and/or ironic/dreamworld"

Group Exercise:
- Have a discussion with the group about positives now and in the future.
- Ask everyone to make a list of all the things they can celebrate about in their current lives and futures. Explain they can be hopes, real, ironic or dreams.
- If you can, put a track on and give them time to do this.
- When you come back together, establish an order and get everyone in the group to say one thing on their list at a time. You could even put some music on to really underline this positive moment as a collective.
- Once you've done this, reflect and choose which ones you'd like to include in the final performance. It could be all of them!

The Pack
by Stef Smith

The Sounds of the Animal

"Is referred to as singular but it can be performed by multiple voices or performers or maybe a different number of people at different moments."

Group Exercise:

- Performers can do this live or you could record it or you could have a combination of both.
- Listen to similar sounds on YouTube with the group and discuss their characteristics.
- Have a think about the style of performance you'd like to make – you can stay literal or push it into an abstract place – choose what works for you.
- One exercise you could use to try and explore the sounds is by making the young people into an orchestra playing the animal noises.
- Think of your hands as batons – perhaps your left hand going up or down indicates volume and your right hand going up or down indicates the breathing transforming into a howl – there's lots of adaptations so think about what works best for you and try things out!
- Play with the differences and you can split the orchestra into sections (e.g. A,B,C,D) so when you shout "Team A", for example, only the young people in Team A voice the noises until you say "full orchestra" and everyone joins in again.
- This allows the young people to start to experiment with the noises in a collective environment and not be fearful of trying things out.
- It also allows you to hear lots of different options and see what works, and what doesn't.

Is This A Fairytale?
by Bea Webster

Kingdom Name

Group Exercise:

- Make a list with the group of all the things that you might find in a kingdom — encourage the group to think outside the box and use their imagination, after all that's what the play is about!
- If online, use a word document and share the screen so everyone can see the list.
- You could explore the kingdom by getting everyone to say a sentence about their favourite part of it. For example, "my favourite part is the huge waterfall" or "my favourite part is the hot air balloons in the sky" or "my favourite part is the floating rainbow rats!". You could even ask them to draw a picture.
- Depending on the group or if you're in the space get groups to make different images or vignettes of their favourite places.
- After you've done some exploring of the Kingdom, you could use your word bank to find the name of it. It could be relatively literal i.e. the Kingdom of Stars or it could add two words (or more!) together i.e. the Kingdom of Castlebeans. Bea the writer encourages that the wilder the name the better!

Trying to Make the Jester Laugh
"All the jesters spend a while trying to make the Princess laugh. Each jester tries a new thing."

Group Exercise:

- Discuss the situation of the princess with the group and how she needs to be cheered up.
- Ask the group — either individually or in groups depending on the context — to come up with one idea of how to make her laugh.
- This doesn't have to be restricted to the Jesters if you want to involve the whole group.
- This should be a fun filled task and a way of generating material which you can choose from to include in the final show.

Ozymandias
by Jack Nurse & Robbie Gordon

Letter Exercise

Talk to the group about the recent news stories regarding the tearing down of statues in town centres and how this relates to what is explored in the play — how the tearing down of statues symbolises a change or shift in history.

Set the group a task to research statues or landmarks in their area and see if they can find any problematic history associated with them.

Hear back from the group what they found out and then set the group the task of writing a letter to their local MP demanding action. (For example, the letter could demand a statue be taken down, to rename a building or street, or to amend a plaque with a footnote about that person's history)

The group could write letters as individuals, in pairs or in small groups — whatever suits how the research part of this task unfolds

Feel free to publicise this action on social media to make more political noise, to demonstrate how your group is taking action and to draw attention to your production!

Familiarisation

Whatever way you have decided to approach the staging of the piece, this point in the process is about embedding all the understanding of the text into the young people and giving them as much confidence in what they are doing as possible.

This part of the process is all about pinning things down – both in terms of ideas and staging (or if this is an online or filmed performance, pinning the nuts and bolts down of how you are going to achieve the end product). A young person might have been trying out loads of accents for a particular knight in Is This A Fairytale? Now a decision must be made on what is the best idea or version of playing that character. It might be that a number of different ways of doing a certain moment have been tried and experimented with – now it is time to choose one of them. You might have made loads of different videos trying out things for a certain moment – now is the moment to decide which ones to use.

One of the hardest parts of rehearsals is trying to learn the lines! Below are a couple of ideas of how to generate familiarisation without losing focus or feeling like a boring exercise. There is also an exercise catering for an online process more focussed on creating video content.

Whisper Line Run
- Great exercise for creating a focus on the words and dialogue only.
- Ask the group to do a line run (where you go through the script only reading out the lines and with no action) but only whispering the words.
- This immediately focuses a group as they have to really listen (especially online!) and creates a hushed and attentive atmosphere.

Cartoon Run
- A fun exercise for pushing the boundaries of the performance.
- Get the group to do a run through of the show but to act as "big" as possible – that means be as bold, as unreserved as possible and pushing the performances to their limits.
- You can then pull back performances from there – that's the top of the spectrum now let's find where the right place is to pitch it for any given young person and character – it is particularly handy to pull people out of their shell and have a bit of fun with the source material.
- This would be a particularly good exercise for Is This A Fairytale?, to push the young people into larger than life performances whilst also learning the lines.

Video Re-draft
- If you have been filming different parts of the performance throughout the weeks and then editing them together, you might be able to create a first draft of the performance.
- If you are building the show in this way there may be a deeper understanding of the work as the time goes on.
- As an exercise you might watch the rough edit privately on YouTube as a group, allowing the cast to think about bits in the performance that they want to re-film now that they are more familiar with the play itself.
- This also allows you as the group leader and director to pass on any notes you have about performances and videos.

Final Performance

Ahead of the final performance you will need to decide what form the play will take. There are a few options we've listed below but the opportunities for creativity are endless and don't feel restricted to anything that is in this handbook:

- You could make loads of short videos and edit them together.
- You could do a live reading on a conference platform like Zoom.
- You could do an outdoor site-specific show that you film live.
- You could even be on stage, in front of a live audience, who knows?

Regardless of the form the performance must adhere to the government guidelines and keep up to date with them as they develop. One thing we do ask is that when finished the final performance or rehearsal is recorded and uploaded to the Positive Stories for Negative Times web page.

8. Film the play

From September 2020 — March 2021, groups are invited to film their play and share it on our Positive Stories for Negative Times website. The final results of the hundreds of groups taking part will be available to view on www.positivestories. scot. Here are some tips and tricks about how to achieve best practice when filming your final performance.

How you do this will depend on the type of production you've gone for. Have you decided to edit videos together? Have you decided to perform live in a space and capture it as a recording? Whichever way you've decided to film your performance, you will need to think about some key things — light, sound, framing and practicalities.

Light

- Light not only defines and focuses the performers but it also sets the tone of a piece, establishes an atmosphere or evokes emotion.
- Experiment with different lighting options and be aware of where your main light source is. Watch out for unintentional shadows on performers' faces and make sure everything you want to be picked up by the camera is effectively lit and in focus.
- One of the main things to remember with light is to avoid having a window or light source behind the performers as you will look "silhouetted" — unless this is an effect you are going for!
- Try to make sure the light source is either facing performers directly or slightly to the side of centre (depending on how you wish the composition to look).
- "Lock off" your exposure on your device so that it doesn't fluctuate when movement happens within the frame. This depends on the device that you're using but on phones you can do this by holding the point on the screen you want to expose until the exposure locks. It'll stop the strange automatic shifts in exposure you often see when someone moves around on screen when filming themselves.

Sound

- Good quality audio is essential for clear, communicative and powerful filming.
- Try to ensure as minimal background noise as possible.
- If young people are performing from home then make sure they are aware of background noise and do their best to mitigate any noises like TVs, washing machines, open windows, people talking etc.
- Plan the timing of filming videos for when the least noise is expected in the location you are filming in.
- If your performance is being filmed outside then watch out for natural noises like wind or traffic — wind in particular will affect the final recording so be careful of this.
- If you have a microphone, or a way to record the audio separately to the video to better quality than a phone or laptop could, we recommend that you do this.
- A handy tip for this is to clap at the beginning of performances/takes so that you can match the separate audio and video files together when editing by pairing the sound and visual of the clap.

Framing

Simple things to consider about framing:

- Think about what shots are going to tell your story best and think about your background.
- If young people are in their home, then they have to make sure the shot is focused and there's not any clutter in the background or objects that audiences will pick up on as having a meaning when you don't want them to.
- A clear background means you can also be selective in what is included in specific shots amplifying the meaning or importance of anything that is included. Examples for each play include:
  - A map for The Pack.
  - A cocktail mixer for Bad Bored Women of the Rooms.
  - An old fairytale book for Is This A Fairytale?
  - The shadow of a statue for Ozymandias.
  - A mug for Hold Out Your Hand.

- If the performance is having to happen from home, remember that this doesn't mean you can't be imaginative with locations and how different spaces can be used in different ways!

- Think about the rule of thirds:
- By definition, the rule of thirds is when you divide an image into thirds using two horizontal lines and two vertical lines. (fig 1)
- Using the rules of thirds effectively means positioning important elements of the shot at these intersection points, producing a much more natural image.
- Off centre composition is pleasing to the eye because it is where our sight goes first.

- Using the rule of thirds, you can also think about the "headroom" of the subject:
- If you watch most TV programmes and films closely, the framing often puts characters' faces in line with the top horizontal line.
- This is because as a general rule, the subject's eyes should be two thirds of the way up the screen ensuring focus and that there is sufficient space between their head and the top of the frame.

(fig 1)

Practicalities

A big one: remember to press record when filming! We are speaking from experience...it is the worst feeling in the world when you think you've done the best performance or take of your lifetime and the record button hasn't been hit.

Also, make sure that you have enough space on your camera, laptop or phone depending on how you are filming the final performance. A quick Google about your device and how much space a certain amount of video takes up will make sure that you know if you need to delete files in order to film the final performance. It is generally good practice to have a wee bit more storage available than you think you'll need, just in case.

9. Upload the play

If you're taking part between September 2020 and March 2021, the next step is to send us your play. Groups will use We Transfer to send their final files to us.

When we receive them, we will put an introduction with the Positive Stories for Negative Times title card as well as opening credits that include your choice of play, the playwright and the name of your group. If you'd like, at the end of the film we can add credits with each young person's first names to create a truly bespoke and celebratory document of your work and process. All of the finished plays will be hosted on www.positivestories.scot

10. Share the work

We want to create as much of a buzz as possible around each individual final filmed performance, so please continue to tag us on social media so we can shout about your work too!

Have a wee think about using Eventbrite or an online ticketing system to create hype and focus for audiences that will watch your final performance. Revisit our section on technology in part two for thoughts in how to do this.

Just a reminder that you are not able to post the finished film on our own platform, it has to come straight to us and then any events you arrange or buzz you want to make on social media will need to link directly to your page on the Positive Stories website. This is due to licensing laws and permissions granted by the writers.

On the Positive Stories website, each group will get an individual watch page with details about your group(s) and their films. There is a like function and comments box underneath so encourage your audiences to interact and feedback on your brilliant work!

When promoting the work please make sure you use the following hashtags so we can share it. You can also follow the hashtags to see who else is participating and what groups are using the same play.

@wonder_fools
@traversetheatre
#WFPositiveStories
#ThePack
#Ozymandias
#IsThisAFairyTale
#HoldOutYourHand
#BadBoredWomen

References and inspirations

As mentioned throughout this book, we are indebted to the many people we have come into contact with during our careers to date whether that be through workshops, collaborations or reading their books. As we mentioned earlier in this handbook, we see ourselves as artistic magpies — cherry-picking what works best for us from all the wonderful practitioners we have come across. Below are a few references and inspirations which you can look into for further research and food for thought.

A Beginner's Guide to Devising Theatre by Jess Thorpe and Tashi Gore

The Frantic Assembly Book of Devising Theatre by Scott Graham and Steven Hoggett

Company Three www.companythree.co.uk

Drama Games for Classrooms and Workshops by Jessica Swale

Playwriting: Structure, Character, How and What to Write by Stephen Jeffreys

Is This A Fairytale?
by Bea Webster

Writer's Note

The "Blank" is where each actor can come up with the name for their own character.

There is no restriction on who can play each character. It is open for all. Currently, all of the characters are they/them pronouns. At the start, when everyone has their own characters, they should adapt the pronouns to their own preferred pronouns.

They can come up the Kingdom name collectively. The wilder it is the better!

Characters

Princess
Knight One
Knight Two
Knight Three
Dragon
Witch
Jesters *(to be divided by several actors. How the lines are divided is up to you)*

Jester (All)   Hello! My name is Jester Blank. (*Repeat for each actor to introduce their chosen Jester name.*)

Jester   We are going to tell you a fairytale.

But first, let's read the fairytales already out there and see what they are like!

All pick up a book and start reading.

Once upon a time . . .

Once upon a time . . .

Once upon a time . . .

This one is about a Princess who wanted a Knight to come and save her.

EWWWWWWW.

This one is about a Princess who needed a true love's kiss to save her.

EWWWWWWW.

This one is about a Princess who wanted to find a Prince to marry her.

EWWWWWWW!

Wait, hold up, hold up! What is wrong with that? Some Princesses want to marry a Prince. Some don't and that's okay. I mean, one day I want to get married!

But it's straight away, without even getting to know the Prince!

What if the Prince is not a nice person?

Oh. Yeah! I never thought about that before!

EWWWWWWW.

Why are all fairytales the same? They all end the same way.

I feel like this doesn't represent all Princesses well at all. I mean, what if the Princess wants to marry another Princess?

What if the Prince wants to marry another Prince?

What if the Princess doesn't need a Knight and can fight for themselves?

What if the Princess is a they? Like, I mean you can be a Prince or a Princess. But what if you don't feel like a Princess or a Prince? Do we need a new term for that? Like . . . erm . . . Princette?

Should we invent a new fairytale?

Should we invent the BEST FAIRYTALE EVER?

Wait . . . Look! There! We have a Princess up in this tower.

It's like in the books!

Do we need to tell her she doesn't need a Knight to save her if she doesn't want to?

That maybe she doesn't need saving at all?

Does that mean we can change the story?

We could come up with a different ending!

*All **Jesters** agrees with each other!*

Right! Are we all ready?

Let's do this!

Let's start with the Princess!

Hey Princess!

HEY PRINCESS!

PRINCESS!

PRINCESS!

*Throw something soft at the tower and the **Princess** emerges from the tower.*

Jester (All)   There's the Princess! Hi there! We are the Jesters!

I am Jester Blank (*Repeat for each* **Jester**.)

Jester   What's your name?

Princess   My name is Princess Blank Blank from the Kingdom of Blank.

Jester (All)   Hello Princess Blank Blank! (*Bows.*)

Princess   Nice to meet you all! So are you all Jesters?

Jester   Yes! We are! The finest comedians in all the Kingdom!

Princess   Oh? In that case, can you please make me laugh, or smile? Please?

Jester   Of course, that is our job! And we are very good at this!

All the **Jesters** *spend a while trying to make the* **Princess** *laugh. Each* **Jester** *tries a new thing!*

Princess (*sighs*)   As I thought. Nothing can make me smile or laugh.

Jester   What was that about?

That was weird.

This has never happened before.

We have always made people laugh!

Princess Blank, would you like to come down to talk to us?

Princess   I won't . . . I mean, I can't come down.

Jester   Oh? Why not?

Princess   Erm . . . uhm . . . (*Thinks.*) Yes! I got it! Because a Great Big Dragon is keeping me in here! I am trapped in the tower! Ahhhhhhh! (*Attempts to fake faint melodramatically.*)

Jester   Oh no!

Gasp!

Dragons are very scary!

They can destroy towns in mere minutes!

They like to eat people for dinner!

We need help in defeating the Great Big Dragon!

Maybe we do need a Knight after all . . .

Why can't we defeat the Dragon?

I mean, we are trying to change the story?

Hmmm . . . that's true . . .

Wait . . . Look! Speak of the devil! The Knights are arriving!

Let's hide and watch what happens first and then we can do something!

HURRY UP!

*The **Jesters** hide quite badly so they are clearly visible but they think they are hiding very well.*

Knight One   HARK, WHO GOES THERE? My name is Knight Blank! I am quite good looking. I am a Great Knight, I won last year's jousting championship! I have defeated many people in the Arena! Is this the Princess's tower? I am here to save the Princess and win her hand in marriage! Then I can become the future King! I have worked my whole life just to rescue the Princess! It is my single, sole purpose! Without that purpose, I am nothing!

Jester   This is your average, stereotypical Knight.

A boring, Plain Knight.

Urgh. They're no good for our story!

We need to tell Knight Blank that there is more to life than Knighting.

The **Jesters** *comes out of hiding.*

There's a whole world to see!

Knight One   What?

Jester   Erm. Like, you don't need to marry the Princess.

Especially if the Princess doesn't want to.

You have other options in life.

Knight One   But this is what I was born to do!

Jester   Nobody is born to do anything!

Knight One   Impossible! I was born to win the Princess's hand!

Jester   Erm . . . Oh, look, another Knight! Let's move on; let's ask that one! Hi! What is your name?

Knight Two   Hi . . . erm . . . My name is . . . Knight . . . Blank . . .

Long pause. **Jesters** *look at each other.*

Knight Two   I dunno what else to say.

Jester   Hi Knight Blank!

Why don't you tell us about you?

Knight Two   Like what?

Jester   Anything?

Knight Two   I have . . . erm . . . I won the best Dungeon Master trophy in the Dungeons and Dragons tournament this year! Does that count?

Jester   I . . . suppose so?

It's a different kind of . . . championship, I guess?

Knight Two   I just bloomin' love Dungeons and Dragons! I'm the most sought after Dungeon Master in all the Kingdom!

Jester   It's a brilliant game!

Knight Two   I just love board games! I also won the Catan championship!

Jester   Wow! That is amazing!

Whispers very loudly to the other **Jesters**.

This is definitely the opposite of your average Knight.

Maybe he could be good for our story?

Yes! That's true! I think Knight Blank woul–

Gets interrupted by **Knight Three** *storming in*.

Knight Three (*storms in like they own the place*)   Peasants, move out of the way! Very, Very Important Knight Arriving! (*Strikes a pose.*) My name is Sir Blank Blank Blank of Blank! I am a wonderful Knight in shining armour! I am the BEST Knight THERE EVER WAS! I HAVE SLAYED MANY, MANY, MANY, MANY, MANY DRAGONS!

Knight Three *shoves a scroll in the* **Jester***'s hand to read out*.

Jester   What is this?

Knight Three   Read from the scroll, minion!

Knight Three *poses throughout the reading*.

Jester   Okay, I will read it . . . Wait, I'm not a minion! I'm not yellow and I don't wear dungarees and –

Knight Three (*interrupting*)   Just read it Jester Blank! I don't want to anger Sir Blank Blank Blank of Blank! Wow, that's a mouthful of a name . . .

Jester   Uhm . . . Okay . . . Here goes . . . Sir Blank Blank Blank of Blank hails from the small town of . . . I can't say the word . . . Ba . . . bo-bon . . . ba . . . bin . . . kin . . . bun . . .

Knight Three   It's Babonbabinkinbun!

Jester   Yes . . . That one! Ba . . . bo . . . ba . . .

Oh just give it to me!

Another **Jester** *takes the scroll and starts reading it.*

Sir Blank has travelled all over the world to prove he is the mightiest Knight there ever was.

Sir Blank has won this year's Jousting Championship, thus replacing Sir Blank (**Knight One**)!

Sir Blank has also defeated many creatures, such as trolls, goblins, wizards, witches, minotaurs, wolves, ogres, orcs, krakens, the Loch Ness Monster . . . is the Loch Ness Monster even real? Anyway . . . hippogriffs, werewolves, gargoyles, yetis . . . Blimey, how long is this? Let's skip to the end, I can't handle anymore!

Long pause to skip to the end of a long scroll.

Sir Blank is the . . . (*Clears throat.*) best Knight there ever was! Thus, they HAVE to marry the Princess and live happily ever after!

Oh this is terrible!

Oh my Goblins. This is really boring!

They've killed so many creatures!

Killing is not good!

That doesn't make a Knight a good Knight!

Knight Three   How dare you all! It is Glorious! I am the BEST Knight there ever was and ever will be!

Knight One   Scandalous! I am the best Knight there ever was and ever will be!

Knight Two   Yes! I mean, no! No! I mean . . . uh . . . I am the best Knight there ever was and ever will be! I think.

All the **Knights** *argue with each other.*

Jester   We need to do something with the Knights!

Otherwise our story won't be any different!

It will be the same as all the other rubbish fairytales!

They're going to ruin it!

No! They can't ruin the story

We need to tell the Knights that there is more than one way to be a Knight!

Hmmm.

I just feel like something is missing.

Me too, actually . . .

Ah! I got it! Isn't this is where a dragon usually appears?

Dragon (**Dragon** *pops in*)   Oh yes! That was my cue! Sorry! I'm terribly late! What am I doing? Oh yes, I need to scare the Knights away from the Princess!

(*Roars weakly.*) There you go!

Knight Three   HA! You call that a roar? RUBBISH! I'm going to take your heart out and turn you into a wand!

ROOOOAAAAAAR!

Knight Two *runs away and hides*.

Jester   HIDE!

RUN AWAY!

This Knight says he has slain many dragons!

He is a dragon killer!

SAVE YOURSELF, DRAGON!

Knight One   Why are you telling the Dragon to run away? Aren't the Knights meant to slay the Dragon? Well, except for Knight Blank (**Knight Two**), who seems to be . . . hiding badly behind that (*whatever the object is*)?

Jester   Because we don't want this to be a stereotypical fairytale story!

Knight One   What?

Knight Three   BAH, COWARDS! ALL OF YOU! AND YOU! You call yourself a Dragon! LOOK AT YOU!

Dragon (*holds back from crying*)   That's really mean!

Knight Three (*tries to take the sword out, but gets stuck for a while before eventually drawing the sword out*)   Come at me, Dragon!

Dragon   Help me! Please save me! HELP ME!

Princess *comes out of the tower and stands in front of the* **Dragon**.

Princess   WHAT IS THIS RUCKUS? WHAT IS GOING ON?

Everyone is very shocked and confused.

Well? What is happening?

Jester   But . . . you left the tower! Aren't you, like, stuck in the tower?

I mean, it's good, because we don't want you stuck in the tower!

This is great!

And the Dragon, well, didn't you say it was . . .

Princess (*interrupts*)   Yes, yes, yes! Right. Well.

I don't know how to break this news to you . . . but . . . I'm here by my own choice. I'm not stuck in the tower or anything.

Knight One   But it is our sacred duty to rescue you!

Princess   Why?

Knight Two   Because . . . erm . . . I know this answer! You are a . . . Princess? Is that right?

Princess   Yes, so?

Knight Three   'Knights'! Look at me and learn from me. This is how it is done. Your Very Royal Highness, the most beautiful Princess Blank Blank of Kingdom of Blank. My name is Sir Blank . . .

Princess   Hurry up, I don't have all day! I heard your name from the tower! I think people from the other side of the kingdom heard you, thank you very much!

Knight Three   Yes, my name is glorious. Your Very Royal Highness, it is because you are a Princess. In the stories, a Princess must be rescued by her true love, and marry them! Or be saved by a true love's kiss!

This is the way of the world, and so it must be done!

Princess   What? No! Those stories aren't real life! I certainly don't need rescuing and I MOST definitely do not want a true love's kiss! As you can see, I am perfectly capable on my own!

Jester   Wait! What about the Dragon?

Princess   What about the Dragon?

Dragon   Hi! I thought I'd introduce myself! How are you all doing? My name is Dragon Blank, of the Blank! It's nice to meet you all!

Jester   Hi Dragon Blank!

Knight One   But I thought Dragons are meant to be big and scary and . . . well . . . you're not . . .

Dragon   What do you mean?

Knight Two   Like . . . erm . . . it's dinner time right now. And you're not chasing after us trying to eat us?

Dragon   Eat people? EWWWWWWWWW. No, thank you. My diet consists entirely of chocolate! It's ravishing! Why would you think that I want to eat people?

Jester   Erm . . . I think it's because you are a Dragon? And it's a well-known fact that Dragons like to eat people . . . Although we think that is boring, and we love the fact that you love chocolate!

Dragon   Yes! Dairy Milk in particular!

Jesters   I'm partial to Galaxy!

Anyway . . . didn't you tell us that the Dragon was keeping you hosta –

Princess (*interrupts*)   Erm . . . about that. Dragon Blank, I'm sorry that I lied that you were keeping me hostage. I shouldn't have lied, and that could have put you in danger. The truth is, Dragon Blank has been helping me.

Knight Three   That can't be true! Wait . . . Dragon Blank has tainted the mind of our Princess! Thus, Dragon Blank needs to be slain!

They go to chase after the **Dragon**.

Knight One *puts their feet forward so* **Knight Three** *trips over them.*

Knight One   Sorry, they were getting on my nerves! Always ask, never draw your sword first!

Knight Two *emerges.*

Knight Two   Is Sir Blank Blank Blank of Blank down? Phew. They are scary!

Dragon   Are you not scared of me?

Knight Two   At first, I was. You're the first real Dragon I've ever met, actually. And you seem nice. But Sir Blank Blank Blank is terrifying!

Knight One   So, you were actually hiding from Sir Blank Blank Blank?

Knight Two   Yes.

Knight Three (*gets up*)   Owww . . . that hurt!

Princess   Thank you. Sir Blank (**Knight Three**), can you just listen please? No more fighting. So . . . if I'm honest, I'm not in a good place, in my head. I can't seem to feel happy. I can't enjoy anything. And my mind is telling me horrible stuff. So Dragon Blank has been helping me out, bringing me food, water and chocolate. Mmm, chocolate. They bring the best chocolate! And they have been keeping people away from me so I can try to get better myself. And if I want to, I ask Dragon Blank to keep me company.

Knight One *and* **Two** *confer.* **Knight Three** *is listening.*

Knight Two   Dragon Blank, erm . . . We all wanted to apologise for saying that you eat humans and saying that you should be scary and mean.

Knight One   We shouldn't have jumped to conclusions. We should have formed our own. You are very nice!

Jester   Isn't this exciting?!

This is already not a usual fairytale!

Let's keep it up!

And don't stereotype anything again, Knights!

Knight One *and* **Two**   Sorry.

Dragon   Thank you, I appreciate it. Oh, oh! Also, I've been escorting a lovely Witch who happens to be a very terrific counsellor to visit the Princess from time to time! They make the best chocolate frogs that jump around! I LOVE THEM!

Jester   Jumping chocolate frogs? That sounds familiar . . .

Knight Three   What, wait?! Counselling! That's nonsense! Wait, a WITCH? Wait, FROGS?

Princess   There's no shame in counselling, Sir Blank Blank Blank. Yes, Witch Blank has been amazing. They are a very good listener, and they offer me advice and tips on managing my mental health! And Witch Blank does put on a good show with their magic, it's very entertaining!

Knight Three WITCHCRAFT! THEY HAVE POISONED YOUR MIND! THEY'RE GOING TO TURN YOU INTO A FROG!

Princess Not again . . .

Knight Two Oh, be quiet you big lumbering oaf!

Knight Three (*taken aback*) W-What?

Knight One Did you just . . . tell Sir Blank Blank Blank to be quiet?

Knight Two Yes! Stop taking up SO MUCH SPACE! Give the rest of us a chance!

Jester Wow! This story is getting even more exciting!

A depressed Princess . . . I mean, it's not good that the Princess is depressed.

But they don't need rescuing or marrying off . . .

And it's good that the Princess is getting help . . .

And that the Witch is helping instead of cursing . . .

And there's a Dragon that's super nice and a friend to the Princess . . .

But now, it's just the Knights that are the problem.

We need to give their story a different ending.

How can we make it different for them?

Hmmmmm.

The **Witch** *skips merrily into the scene.*

Jester Ooh, the Witch!

Maybe the Witch will change it up!

We already know that the Witch is not your typical Witch!

Let's watch this unfold first!

Witch   Hello, my darling Princess! How are you doing? (*Looks at everyone.*) Wow! What an audience you have today!

Dragon   Hey Witch Blank!

Witch   Oh, hello there Dragon Blank! Keeping the Princess company as usual?

Princess   Oh, darling Witch Blank! I'm so glad to see you here! You couldn't have arrived at a better time!

Pause as the **Knights** *register the whole scene.*

Knight Three   AHHHHHHHHHHH! IT'S A WITCH!

Knight One   Sir Blank Blank –

Knight Three   THEY'RE GOING TO TURN US INTO FROGS!

Knight One   OH NO!

Knight Two   NO! I DON'T WANT TO BE A FROG!

All the **Knights** *go and hide.*

Princess   NOT AGAIN!

All of the **Jesters** *give out a big sigh.*

Witch   What? Frogs?

Jester   Well, if I were to guess, it's a popular myth that witches turn people into frogs.

Princess   Oh, those old kinds of stories! They're obviously made up!

Witch   Oh what a load of tosh! Nonsense! Twaddle!

Jester   That seems to be the recurring theme.

Witch   Urgh. Stereotypes. I hate them.

Dragon   Me too! The Knights seemed to think I like eating humans!

Witch Oh dear, oh dear. These stories are getting out of hand! It reminds me of Frankenstein's Monster, and the monster isn't a monster after all. What a surprise.

Princess And the Knights seem to think I need to be saved or to be married off.

Knights, please come out?

*All the **Knights** slowly emerge from their hiding place.*

Princess I am not going to marry any of you. I don't need saving by any of you. What I do need is to carry on with Witch Blank and get better.

Knight One But what am I going to do if I cannot win your hand?

Princess There are a lot of things to do!

Jester There's the whole wide world to see!

Knight One Wow . . . I never even thought about that . . . I was made to think otherwise . . .

Knight Two Ooh! I don't want to be a Knight anymore! I felt like I had to because everyone expected me to be one and I felt like I couldn't let anyone down! But being a Knight is Very Scary Business! *(Shudders.)*

Witch Yes! You should do what makes you happy!

Princess And what about you, Sir Blank Blank Blank of Blank?

*Everyone looks at **Knight Three**.*

Knight Three So . . . uh . . . Witch Blank . . . Could I, I'm embarrassed to say this . . . I dunno . . . seek your help? I mean, I love being a Knight . . . but maybe . . . I dunno . . . I think I need help. I also lied when I said I've slain many creatures and people, but . . . it's not true. I felt I had to say it in order to fit in with people . . .

Witch   Of course! There's nothing embarrassing about seeking help! We can set up an initial meeting first and see if we are a good match! Finding the perfect counsellor is the most important thing so that you feel safe and you get the best help possible! And if I'm not right, there are loads of counsellors in the Kingdom of Blank!

Knight Three   Th-Thank you. Then . . . I can take my time to decide what I want to do afterwards? There's no time limit, right?

Jester   That's right! That's a very good start Sir Blank Blank Blank!

So, Knight Blank and Sir Blank, what are you both going to do? Have you thought about it?

Knight One   You were right. This can't be my only purpose. I think I'll travel the world like what you all suggested. Maybe start my own travel book and inspire others to travel! But this time I'll keep an open mind. Like, if I encounter a Goblin or a Giant, I'll speak to them first instead of drawing swords.

Knight Two   I'm going to . . . maybe set up a . . . No, I will set up a Dungeon and Dragons themed hotel! I'm going to call it Knight Knight! Like . . . night night? Get it?

Only the **Dragon** *bursts out laughing, and laughs for a while before stopping.*

Dragon   Ahem. I mean. Can I come with you, Sir Blank? I've always wanted to play Dungeon and Dragons too but nobody let me! Heh. I am a Dragon.

Knight Two   I'd love for you to join me!

Witch   Right Princess Blank, are you ready for our session?

Princess   I am! Everyone, when I am ready to emerge from the tower, I will do so in my own time. I don't need rescuing. I've got Witch Blank and my very loyal friend, Dragon Blank for now. I need to focus on myself first. Then I can be the best Princess I could possibly be, and help people in our wonderful Kingdom! And when I am ready, we can meet up! I'd love to get to know all of you.

Jester   Wow!

What an ending.

Although, like a typical fairytale, this has a happy ending!

What?

Were you expecting something else?

This is a fairytale after all!

Otherwise this wouldn't be a fairytale!

But some of the fairytales out there are actually grim . . .

And Grimm! Get it? No?

You're right! This is not that type of fairytale!

We can make this one a happy ending!

But not your typical ending!

Anyone can rewrite their own stories!

The Princess is getting all the help they need, and now they are surrounded by supportive friends!

The Dragon and Sir Blank decided to open the Knight Knight hotel together, and it was a roaring success!

Sir Blank Blank Blank has now renamed themselves as just Sir Blank. They are now training to become a counsellor!

Knight Blank is now known as the Travelling Knight, documenting people's lives. Knight Blank is very interested in telling other people's stories.

And the Witch . . . Well, the Witch is still a counsellor, helping out people and creatures all over the Kingdom! And they love it.

There you go! Isn't it wonderful!

And for us Jesters?

What was in this for us?

We're going to write about this and then perform this story to everyone else!

I think it is the Best Fairytale Ever!

Hopefully we can tour to the West End!

Maybe win a lot of awards!

I think we would all be amazing actors!

Hmmm . . . how do we end this?

Let's all link arms and skip out of here!

Then come back for the applause.

Then leave the stage?

How's that?

All   The End!

Hold Out Your Hand
by Chris Thorpe

Writer's Note

A text for as many people as there are. Say it in your own voices. Join the lines end to end when they need it. When it says 'silence', don't be afraid to take your time, but remember all silences aren't as long as each other. When the text asks you to share something personal – only go as far as you feel comfortable going – the safer and more confident you feel, the better this works.

Hey

Hey there

Hey

My name's (*name*)

Say that again

We're talking over each other

Let's take turns, just this once

Silence. Then in perfect unison.

Hey

My name's –

Everyone's names in perfect unison.

My name's

Everyone's name, one after the other.

Silence.

This is a play

Kind of

Also not a play

Let's not worry about what this kind of thing's called

What we might have started to call it

This thing we've always done

When we get together

Whatever we've started to call 'together'

And some of us watch and listen

And some of us speak and listen

Whatever we're calling this right now

This is one of those

It's meant to take place

Wherever it takes place

It's meant to take place

Gesture to the other screens/the room.

Here

Which could mean you're wherever you are

And everyone else is wherever they are

Joining together our 'here's' to make a single 'here'

Bolting them edge to edge on a screen

Like self-assembly plastic storage boxes

For human heads

[*The bit between these square brackets is an optional section you can use if everyone's performing remotely –*

And if that's true

Then let's tell you about

Our own worlds outside these boxes

I'm in (*what town or room are you in?*) and it's (*one word to describe it*)

The optional section ends here.]

Or, maybe even, just maybe

That we're all in the same big box

All in the same air

That I can look you in your actual eye

Your actual human glistening, sticky-to-the-touch, see-it-blink *human eye*

Imagine that, if that's not what we're doing

If we're still at the heads-in-boxes stage

Imagine us all in that space, how it's going to feel

When it finally happens

Cos it *will* happen

And if it has happened

If we *are* all together in a room

With air and eyes, and all the sounds

The small sounds of bodies that microphones don't notice

And speakers don't transmit

Take a moment to think back to the time

That lost age, of months or weeks or even just days ago

When we couldn't do this

When our bodies were quiet

Or at least made noises only we could hear

When maybe the only clue to our actual existence

Our real world existence

Was when we froze, or glitched

Or had to leave and return while we stayed in the exact same place

Long silence.

Weird, isn't it

How whatever you're doing now

How whatever way we're doing this now

Can so quickly become the only way to do it

The only way we've ever done it

I guarantee you, even though

Even though some things might be different

The distance between us, if we're in a room

The tension in the room that was never there before

Or the lag of different broadband speeds

The colour and closeness of the walls around us

We'll still find it hard to imagine

That we used to do this any other way

Or that the way we're doing it will change

Silence.

Anyway

This play, this thing, this poem

What we're calling what's happening doesn't matter

But it has a name, apart from that

And the name of it is

Hold Out Your Hand

Silence.

That's what was printed

At the top of the document they gave us

It was in bold, to seem important

To say, this is the title

Silence.

But we're not so into that

Hold Out Your Hand

We're not that into it

Silence.

I mean, we get it, we're not

We're not stupid, we get

That someone thought it sounded hopeful

About connection, and contact

But it's a bit thin, isn't it

A bit on the bland side

A bit full of the kind of

The kind of empty optimism that's

Just meant to get us through this

Like something you'd say to a child

Crossing a road, or maybe

Walking down unfamiliar streets to a funeral

Or something, feels kind, but unfocused

Almost as if it was a compromise

Like the guy thought – I want to make something

About getting through this, but just that

Not about *doing* but about *being there*

About *reassurance* and how everything is

Going to be OK

How *if we are just here for each other*

Everything is going to be OK

So, Hold Out Your Hand, he thought

That'll do – except, it won't

It could have been – and this is no disrespect

Honestly mate, we're saying these words aren't we –

No disrespect but

It could have been a better title

What about – The Forgotten Months

Or – Head in a Box

Or – This Street Has Never Been So Silent

Or (*list all the titles you can come up with that would be better*)

Something that says clearly

What's happened and the many shades

Of feeling, from relief to joy

To the deepest sorrow to total fury

It's possible to feel about it

And whoever wrote this, for example

I mean I'm sure – it's a man isn't it?

Yeah it's a man

I'm sure he would agree

That there's no way he can really get in our heads

There's a lot he doesn't know

A lot he doesn't want to guess

A lot he thinks, but he knows is wrong

And the rest of it, he's making up

He wouldn't know, how could he

That the lowest point of this year for me was

The worst moment one of you remembers most clearly about 2020 so far – it can be a different moment from a different person every performance.

And the highest point for me was

The best moment one of you remembers most clearly about 2020 so far – it can be a different moment from a different person every performance.

I mean, how could he know that?

But anyway, here we are

Probably, when this is happening

When we're saying this

When you're hearing this

We're still all a bit spooked

Still a bit scared of touching each other

Everyone just feeling a little bit

Like we've been walking down a corridor

That's lined with cheap carpets

And we're about to touch a door handle

Most of us have learned

To move through our own lives like ghosts

As the world changed around us

In ways it never has before

Ways that we had to find words to describe

It was like the door slamming shut behind you

And realising you're not locked out

You're locked *in*

No, that's not it

It was like a montage in a film

Except instead of moving the story on

It repeated the same few frames over and over

No, that's not it either

It was like waiting for a bus, except

The timetable was blank

And all the numbers on the board kept changing

I think we should try this one ourselves

It was like (*what was it like for you?*)

It was like (*what was it like for you?*)

It was like (*what was it like for you?*)

Silence.

That's what it was like

Maybe it still is

Silence.

So

Silence.

Anyone else been having really weird dreams?

Silence.

Don't worry

We're not going to tell you about our dreams

Except, I had this dream –

We literally just said

We literally just said this wasn't going to happen

Just one, let me tell you just one

Silence.

OK

One sentence about a dream one of you had in the last few months.

No that's not it

One sentence about a dream one of you had in the last few months.

That's not it either

One sentence about a dream one of you had in the last few months.

Look, I know this guy's no good at titles

But maybe, just maybe

He can give us a shared dream to tell you

Maybe we can trust him that much

To give us one useful dream

Silence.

It's worth a try

Silence.

So, I had this dream where

I was walking, outside

But it wasn't *my* outside

As in, not what I'd see if I went out the door

It was an outside that differed

In certain very important respects

From anywhere I'd normally find myself

It was huge, for one thing

Not streets or houses

The sky not just a ribbon stretched out over a road

Glimpsed between the artificial horizons

Made by buildings closing in on either side

It was bigger, even

Than landscapes without buildings

Wider than moorland

More distant than the glimpse you get sometimes

Of distant hills

The ground was flat

Not grass-flat, or rock-flat

Or artificial car-park flat

But the flat of an afternoon

Spent looking out of a window

At a leafless winter tree

And the ground the colour of

The light fading on a wasted day

And the sky thrown over

Like an over-washed bed sheet

And the sun invisible

Light just seeming

To come from every direction

No shadows, no bright

And me, not even in the middle of this

Cos there is no middle

If you can't see the edges

Just there, like, in my body

I was definitely in my body

I was absolutely definitely me

Wearing my clothes

My height, my hair, my skin

Standing on that empty ground

In a colourless dream version

Of my everyday shoes

I stood there for a long time

Silence.

Is that it? Is that the dream?

No, I was just doing a long time

Sorry

It's OK – I stood there for a long time

Silence.

And I thought

Do you ever think in dreams?

It's *really difficult*

But I thought

The world's gone

And then I thought about

If that was true –

And at that moment it felt true –

Then really, what's been lost?

I didn't really feel grief

I didn't really feel happiness

There were many things I'd miss

But there were many things I was glad to lose

I guess it kind of balanced out

Into a state of mind

That felt like the landscape looked

I was sad to lose being in some part of a city

On my own, feeling not knowing

Feeling unknown

But I was glad to lose the eyes of strangers on me

I was glad to lose having to think about

How I was going to dress

The worry of what might be thought of me

But I was sad to lose a reason to get dressed at all

I was sad to lose some kinds of touch

But I was glad to lose some other kinds of touch

I was (*something you were glad to lose, or sad to lose*)

I was (*something you were glad to lose, or sad to lose*)

I was (*something you were glad to lose, or sad to lose*)

I was (*something you were glad to lose, or sad to lose*)

But most of all, I think it was control

I was sad to lose control

It was like the whole world

Was a mug that had just been dropped

You know that moment

When you've just made a drink

And everything's right in your life

Then for some reason

For some completely stupid reason

The mug's not in your hand

And your fingers flash through empty air

And for a frozen fraction of a second

The whole thing's laid out before you

There's nothing you can do

But watch its spinning progress to the floor

Well the way you feel in that moment

Like a bystander at an accident

Except the accident's your life –

That's the way the dream felt

Standing there in all that emptiness

Except –

Except – and this is important

Except this isn't real life

In real life the mug was dropped

Somewhere unknown, the other side of the world

Nature had made us a cup of tea

And we'd fumbled it

We were standing in the Universe's kitchen

Watching everything we'd carried

Fall tumbling to the tiles

Who knew the Universe had a tiled floor eh?

Caught in a frozen moment

Of not knowing

Waiting to see if the rules we lived by

The structures we thought were solid

So much we'd forgotten they were there

Waiting to see if they would break or bounce

Out of our control

Nothing we could say

To stop the fall

But, in the dream, in this strange world

The falling, the feeling of it

Was not an action taken or not taken

Was not an accident

Was not the world happening without me

I realised as I stood there

It was a choice

In the dream there was a feeling

That I had no control

But I was in control of it

Of the feeling of not being in control

Which meant I could choose

I could choose not to feel it

It was just me

No rules, no landscape

No buildings, no rocks

No responsibilities no work to do

Everything waiting, everything suspended

And only me there, meaning

No matter what my life

Outside the dream was like

Everything in it was my choice

Silence.

And I wasn't used to that

I was not used to that at all

Silence.

I stood there, just waiting

Waiting for something to happen

Silence.

And slowly it crept up on me

Fearful, yeah, but also kind of thrilling

Nothing was going to happen

Nothing was going to happen

Nothing was going to happen

Unless I made it happen

Silence.

And so

I held out my hand

Oh right that's the title

Makes sense I guess but I still don't like it

Anyway, I held out my hand

Silence.

And absolutely nothing happened

Silence.

I guess I thought once I realised

That what happened was in my power

I'd figured it would come easy

Like, hold out your hand and

Bam – there's a – what

Bam there's a – fountain

A fountain?

I don't know, it was the first thing I thought of

A *fountain*?

OK, bam, there's a (*what?*)

Bam, there's a (*what?*)

Bam, there's a (*what?*)

I think I thought it'd just *flow*

Like film-magic, like game-magic

Like the power in me was point and click

But it didn't

I had to really think about it

I had to start off simple

Which seemed a bit unfair

It was *my* dream after all

But apparently I didn't make the rules

I collected myself

I held out my hand

I started simple

And I thought

Blue, it doesn't get more simple than that

Blue of sky, I thought

And I closed my eyes, and I opened them

And something had almost happened

There was still flatness

Still nothing, but maybe, just maybe

It was a slightly bluer nothing than before

Thing is, I could feel the power

Like a spring inside me

Both kinds of spring I mean

The water kind and the metal kind

Like it was gushing out

But also winding up

And the way to be in charge

Of both those things at once

Was to use them both, think simple

Think 'blue', let it flow out

But also keep the tension, the direction

By answering the question – what kind?

I thought – blue – but this time thought

The blue of the sky

And not just any sky, all skies are blue

But the blue of a sky seen in summer

When you've been up all night

Maybe you've climbed up on a roof

You're the highest point in your surroundings

And the horizon you can see

Knows the sun's on its way

But not for a while

No clouds or anything

No lights on in any of the houses

And just at the end of the dark

There's a blue that says the morning's coming

That blue, I thought, that one

And I held out my hand

And I stretched my fingers wide

Closed my eyes, opened my eyes

And the blue in my head was the whole world

And the world was still simple

Featureless and flat

But that hopeful gentle blue of almost-morning

Was laid across it and within it

Like it had always been there

And it felt strange

This is all sounding a bit weird I know

This is all sounding like some mystical experience

But it wasn't that, it wasn't

The strange feeling of magic, of fantasy

Of extra dimensions and portals

Of alien worlds opening up

It was the strangeness of *this* world

Even this simple world

This simple landscape from inside me

Being within my control

Being mine to command

One decision that was mine

Silence.

And then?

It was a dream

Yeah I know it was a dream

What happened then?

I woke up

Silence.

Same room

Same room in the same house

Same house on the same street

Same street in the same town

Same town in the same country

Same river flowing into the same sea

Same carpet, same curtains that don't quite close

Same splash of paint on the back of the door

Same clothes in the same pile

Same sun at the same angle

Lighting up the same spot on the same poster

Same sounds from outside

Same voices from inside

Same voice inside me

Same day repeating again and again

Same planet crawling through the same space

Same screen in my hand telling me

The same half-fake information

The same hysterical guesswork

The same words spilling from the same faces

The same opinions on the same subjects

The same arguments over the same action

The same stale food chewed over

By the same tired mouths

While the same stale power

Grasped in the same stale hands

Thrummed in the background

Like the noise of a distant factory

Silence.

Turns out the way the dream feels

It isn't a dream

Silence.

And this is what I think we're here to say

As far as I can tell

That feeling, being swept up

In events you can't control

As the weather patterns change

And the hospitals fill up

And the future you wanted

Seems to melt under your hands

Being swept up in all that, in your smallness

But at the same time being so very still

It's not some imaginary landscape

It's the way life feels right now

In a year from now (*what do you want in a year from now?*)

In a year from now (*what do you want in a year from now?*)

In a year from now (*what do you want in a year from now?*)

And now, right now

Not the day that some guy is writing these words

Late at night in a corner of some far city

But right now

In this room

Or through this screen in all these rooms

That future world still feels untouchable

We're not despairing

Please don't think that we're despairing

We're just saying

Parts of the life we want

Still feel like dreams

Still feel lost in a landscape

We're standing in, wondering what happens next

Silence.

But we remember

We're still remembering

The spring

And the spring

The power to hold tight

And the power to let go

How in the dream we knew

That the world didn't just act on us

We could act on it

That there's a focus we can find

Inside ourselves

And then, together

Silence.

Hold out your hand

There's power in it

Hold out your hand

Silence.

I still don't like that title

I know, but we've come this far

And anyway, we've not just been handed it

We can do what we like

We can make whatever this is

We can make it into something of our own

Carry on, on our own terms

Are you ready?

Silence.

Here goes

Silence.

Whether we're saying these words

While we breathe the same air

Or we look at different screens

Whether we've come miles to be together

Or we're miles apart and all together

If we can't say

What we want this world to be

Then we're alone

Trapped in our own dreams

Silence.

Hold out your hand

This is how it starts

The trick of it

Is realising we don't have to dream it

Hold out your hand

Let it break out of the landscape

Through the edge of the monitor

Through the distance between us

Touch doesn't have to be touch

To still count as connection

Hold out your hand

We're still in the dream

Still in that landscape, even when we're awake

Feeling alone, lost in it

No markers to guide us

No roads to guide us

No history to guide us

But

Hold out your hand

Feel the power in it

Remind yourself this land

This uncharted land

Is yours as much as anyone's

Put a marker in the ground

Doesn't have to be nearby

Somewhere you'd like to be

A year from now

Something you'd like to achieve

Ten years from now

Some change you'd like to see

Tomorrow

Doesn't matter

The important thing is

It starts with you

The important thing is

Even in these times of isolation

Even in these times of confusion

Even in these times of repetition

Even in these times of repetition

There is togetherness, and change

And there is choice in what we do with it

One decision that is mine

And a choice to share it

So we're sharing this

(*Something to keep*)

(*Something to let go of*)

(*Something to keep*)

(*Something to let go of*)

(*Something to keep*)

(*Something to let go of*)

(*Carry on until you've said everything you want to*)

So

What do we do now?

The Pack
by Stef Smith

'Solitude is the profoundest fact of the human condition. Man is the only being who knows he is alone, and the only one who seeks out another.'

Octavio Paz

'Loneliness is a sign you are in desperate need of yourself.'

Rupi Kaur

Writer's Note

This is a play for two or two hundred performers, and everything in-between.

The lines can be divided as the production sees fit as long as different performers take alternate lines, denoted by the dash (–).

A forward slash (/) means the next performer interrupts the line before.

For ease and clarity, the animal in the script is referred to as singular but it can be performed by multiple voices or performers or maybe a different number of people at different moments.

This play reads like one long moment but let it build, pause and have breath. Almost like a wave, rushing into shore then slowly retreating, with each wave building until it reaches land.

There are few stage directions, imagine it as you wish.

Scratching.

Scurrying.

Sniffing.

Scratching.

Scurrying.

Something behind me.

One foot, then another.

One foot, then another.

The rustle of something not far away.

Scratching.

Scurrying

Sniffing.

Scratching

Scurrying.

Something behind me.

One foot, then another.

One foot, then another.

The rustle of something not far away.

Stop.

Turn around to nothing.

There is nothing behind me, next to me, near me.

Nothing.

A branch snaps.

- And my heart jumps into my throat and before I know it – it's one foot, then another. Quicker now. One foot, then the other. Quicker now. The sound of breathing. Inhale. Exhale. Inhale. Exhale. Quicker now. Quicker and quicker again. Inhale. Exhale. All I can hear is my breath. All I can see is darkness. Trusting my feet. Trusting my breath. Quicker now. Trusting my body to throw itself forwards. Towards the darkness, the nothingness. Trusting my body to move.

- Keep breathing.

- Keep breathing.

- Keep breathing.

- My heart is exploding in my chest.

- Boom.

- Boom.

- Boom.

- My heart is exploding in my chest.

- Boom.

- Boom.

- Boom.

- Until I . . .

- Until I . . .

- I can't.

- Until I can't.

- I can't do it anymore.

- My heart.

- My throat.

- My body exhausted.

- I can't move anymore. Try to catch my . . .

- Inhale. Exhale.

- Try to catch my . . .

- Something was there.

- Inhale. Exhale.

- But now it's not.

- My heartbeat in my ears.

- Inhale. Exhale.

- All I can hear is my heartbeat in my ears.

- Ba-Boom.

- Ba-Boom.

- Ba-Boom.

- My palms. Sweaty and sticky. Wet with worry. I don't know how I got here; I don't know how I'm going to get out. My heartbeat in my ears. My stomach in my throat. Nothing is where it should be. And I don't know how I got here.

- Nothing is where it should be.

- Breath.

- Just breath.

- I've lost my phone. My diary was discarded days ago. There are no maps for places like this.

- Stomach growls.

- Skin twitches and itches.

- Somehow both still and shaking.

- Somehow totally lost.

- Somehow utterly alone.

–   But if I could just get to where I am going too. I'll be okay. If I could just get there. If I could just . . .

The performer notices the sound of someone or something breathing.

–   What was . . .

–   What was that?

–   Who's there?

The breathing gets louder and fills the space. It is unsettling. We cannot see the animal; we don't know how close it is or if it will kill or comfort.

–   What's that?

–   Who's there?

–   What's that?

–   You okay?

–   I just . . .

–   You had the TV blaring.

–   Oh, sorry. I just wanted to make sure I didn't miss anything important . . . I'll turn it down. Sorry.

–   It's okay. You want anything from the kitchen?

–   No. I'm okay. Thanks. What you up to?

–   Just sorting out my room.

–   Cool.

–   Was I being noisy?

–   No, not at all. Can barely hear you.

Silence.

–   You sure you're okay? You look a little – serious.

–   I'm fine. Just – concentrating.

–   I'll leave you to it then, see you in a bit.

- See you.

- Oh, meant to say – do you fancy hanging out with some mates later? Thought we could all catch up. Have a laugh. Kill some time. Maybe you can get into a deep and meaningful. Share some secrets. Go on. It's been ages since you've hung out with everyone. You know you want too. Deep down – you know you want to.

- Sure. Sounds . . . fun.

- Great. See you in a bit.

- See you in a bit.

- See you.

- See you.

- See.

- You.

The words slowly turn into the sound of breathing.

Inhale. Exhale.

The sound and feeling grows.

- Scratching.

- Scurrying.

- One foot in front of the other.

- This feeling – just here in the centre of my chest.

- Not a feeling – an absence of feeling.

- My heart beats. My heart aches.

- One foot in front of the other.

- Scuff the mud on the floor that becomes the carpet that becomes floorboards that becomes foundations that becomes the ground again.

- A world covering a world covering a world.

- The trees become leaves become patterns on the wallpaper, becomes the forest again.

- A world covering a world covering a world.

- The swirls on the ceiling become the sky, becomes the ceiling again.

- A world covering a world.

The animal quietly growls. Threatening.

The performer acknowledges it, they feel like they are being watched. They try to distract themselves.

- Breath.

- Just breath.

- Focus.

- Fidget. Fingers flick and click.

- The TV is lit with light that dances aimlessly along my eyes.

- Flick and click.

- I don't know where my phone is and it's probably out of battery or signal or something.

- Probably smashed it.

- Probably dropped it hours ago.

- Probably just stuck behind the couch.

- I don't know where I am. If I could just get to where I am going too. I'll be okay. If I could just get there.

- Wanting the direction of desire.

- The focus of having time filled.

- Wanting.

- Longing.

- No hard corners in the day anymore.

- Sunrise and sunset is the best I can get. My chests pulls itself, stretchy and stringy and thin.

- An abundance of anger with no aim and no action.

- Floats in me. Flattens me.

- A forest of thoughts.

- Full and unfilled. All at /

- Are you nearly ready? We will be late at this rate.

- Sorry. I was just . . . sorry.

- Cat got your tongue.

- No. No. I just feel quiet.

- Fair enough. Because when life gives you lemons.

- It does exactly what it says on the tin.

- Because home is where the heart is.

- There is always a silver lining. Through thick and thin. Throw down the gauntlet.

- Voices and hand gestures and faces and sounds.

- Fighting tooth and nail.

- Bite the head off.

- A smooth sea never made a skilled sailor.

- Let's drain the swamp.

- Voices and hand gestures and faces and sounds and conversations, like crows, that flutter around me, not with me, not through me, around me. Wings. Waves. Wanting. Feel like I've hovering above myself, watching a puppet play out the performance. All these people and yet I forget. I've forgotten how to do this. No, not forgotten. I don't know how; I don't know how to get out of the forest of my own thoughts.

–   You're looking – well.

–   Thanks.

–   Not seen you online much.

–   Leaves rustle. Branches bend and break.

–   Will you reply to my text when you get a second?

–   Crickets call out.

–   Let me know if you fancy doing something?

–   The sound of rain.

–   Have you been busy?

–   Yeah. Yeah, really busy.

–   What you been up to?

–   Been going for walks. Lots of walks. There is this forest and – been going there. Nearly every day, actually.

–   I'm not that into walking. I get bored too easily.

–   Yeah. Suppose some folk do.

–   It's meant to be good for you though, isn't it? All that fresh air.

–   Yeah. Meant to be good for you.

–   Leaves rustle. Branches bend and break.

–   The sound of rain.

–   Crickets call out.

–   I cracked my compass and the arrow arm swirls, aimlessly. Never pointing north for longer than a nanosecond. A little earthquake line up the glass. Smooth to the touch but the cracks are underneath. In the body of the mechanism. The cracks are on the inside.

–   That was fun wasn't it?

– Sure.

– We'll have to do it again soon.

– Sure.

– One foot in front of the other.

– Scuff the mud on the floor that becomes the carpet that becomes floorboards that becomes foundations that becomes the ground again.

– A world covering a world covering a world.

– The trees become leaves become patterns on the wallpaper, becomes the forest again.

– A world covering a world covering a world.

– The swirls on the ceiling become the sky, becomes the ceiling again.

– A world covering a world.

– I need to find my way of out of this, I want to find my way out of this, but I don't know where to turn. I lift up my laptop. Diving into the digital dirt and begin to dig.

– And dig.

– And dig to find answers and questions and reasons and options and opinions and I dig.

– Click. Scroll. Tap. Type.

– Slip. Trip. Walk. Run.

– Click. Scroll. Tap. Type.

– Trying to find my way out of this, trying to dig my way out of this.

– Deeper and deeper into the digital dirt.

– Answers and questions and reasons and options and opinions.

- A minefield of murmurs and mirrors.
- Worms and worries wriggle around me. My chest echoes with anger and angst.
- Still but shaking.
- Click. Scroll. Tap. Type.
- Eyes blur with tiredness and the brightness of screens.
- The bright blue blur of digging deeper.
- Answers and questions and reasons and options and opinions.
- This grasping in me has grown. Grabbing at things. Something to fill me.
- Something to satisfy the hunger.
- So, I add to basket.
- In fact, add three of those to basket.
- Something to fill me.
- Something to satisfy the hunger.
- Add to basket.
- Something to wear.
- Something to watch.
- Something to click and flick.
- Something to fill me.
- Add to basket.
- Proceed to check out.
- Grabbing at things.
- Proceed to check out.
- Grasping and groping.

The animal snarls.

– Take my money.

– Currency conversion from pounds into dollars into euros into yen.

The animal barks.

– Take my money.

The animal barks and snarls over the next moments of dialogue. It builds and builds, almost drowning out the words of the play.

– From yen into euros into dollars into pounds.

– The bite and crunch and the jaws of money, all these things I own. The teeth of taking things. All these things I own.

– Personalised adverts. Prescriptions for pacifying.

– All these things I own. All these things that own me.

The animal stops. Silence.

– What are you buying?

– Nothing.

– I can see it on your laptop, what you wasting money on?

– It's not a waste.

– More packages came this morning. All with your name.

– Thanks.

– Thought you were saving?

– I am.

– More packages came this morning. All with your name.

– Thanks.

– What you buying?

– Add to basket.

−   You know you could ask for some of this for your
    birthday?

−   Add to basket.

−   Don't you already have one of those?

−   Add to basket.

−   Do you think you should go to bed?

−   A branch snap. A breath that isn't mine.

−   Something is moving closer.

−   The pad of a paw or a claw or a foot.

−   Closer now.

The animal howls.

*Silence follows, the performer is waiting for the howl again but it
never comes.*

−   All of this will pass and what comes next will happen
    before I know it's even happening.

−   Maybe stillness is the answer.

−   If I stop and stay, quiet and still.

−   Still and darkness are an intoxicating mix it can cuddle
    or kill you. Everything is so inverted that you turn
    yourself inside out. Feel your fragile organs on the
    outside. Nothing is in the right place.

−   Strip light of the kitchen with the clatter of cutlery.

−   Toast. Roast. Crunch and eat. Binge to hide the
    boredom.

−   Toast. Roast. Crunch and eat. Binge to hide the
    boredom.

−   Stuff.

−   Stuff it down.

- No hard corners in the day, everything has become so soft, so lacking in lines.

- Stuff.

- Stuff it down.

- I don't know where I am.

The animal howls again. Silence.

- It's getting late. I'm thinking of going to bed.

- Okay.

- I could stay up if you /

- It's okay. I'm fine.

- You watching something?

- Yeah.

- You staying up?

- Yeah. I'm not tired.

- Restless?

- Yeah. Maybe. I'll turn the light off when I'm done.

- Okay. There some leftovers in the kitchen for you, if you want.

- I've already eaten, thanks.

- Don't stay up too late. You'll turn into a nocturnal animal at this rate.

- An owl.

- When was the last time you went to bed before me?

- A bat. A rat.

- You'll end up sleeping the day away.

- A fox. A coyote.

- Do you know what I really think you should go to bed? I really think /

- I think I can do what I want.

Silence.

- No need to talk like that to me.

- No need to tell me what to do.

- What's wrong with you?

- Nothing.

- I'm trying to help.

- I'm fine.

- You know I'm going to stop asking if you don't /

- I said I'm fine.

Silence.

- Then I'll leave you to it.

Silence.

- Scratching.

- Scurrying

- Sniffing.

- Scratching.

- Scurrying.

- Something behind /

- My phone.

- Charge. Restart. Reset.

- No new messages. The noise of nothing.

- The sound of silence.

- And crickets calling out.

- Photos and messages and updates. Reply and reduce everything down to a snapshot. Reply and reduce everything down to 280 characters or less.

- Here. Take more. More of everything. More photos. More messages. More of me. Here. Take it.

- Binge to hide the boredom.

- More of me there, less of me here. More of me there. Less of me here.

- Who is there?

- Just add to the noise.

- What's that?

- Turn it all up to top volume.

- Who is there?

- This feeling – just here in the centre of my chest.

- Not a feeling – an absence of feeling.

- My heart beats. My heart aches.

- Keep breathing.

- Anger. It's probably anger. I feel like I should be angry at something.

- Hunger. It's probably hunger.

- It's a want. A need. I'm just in the clutch of craving.

- Maybe it's sadness. Grief. But there is nothing, to attach it too. No anchors to acknowledge. Nothing of note to grieve.

- A needling feeling in my ribs. Arms feel like an excess. A bumbling body.

- Tumbling through a forest. Being chased by claws and thorns.

– I feel wired and tired.

– A broken compass.

– Restless.

– Keep breathing.

– I don't know what to do.

– Where to go.

– Or how to leave this place.

– Keep breathing.

– Scratching.

– Scurrying.

– And I want to leave this place.

– I want to leave this place.

– I want to leave this place.

– Please let me leave.

– Please leave me alone.

– Please leave me alone.

– Because maybe I'm scared.

– Maybe that is what this is in me. It's fear.

– I think I might be . . .

The animal howls.

It continues to howl, bark and growl.

The sound builds and builds. Everything is the animal; it overwhelms and engulfs everything.

Then silence.

– Hi.

– You're back?

- I was lying in bed and thought I can't leave you down here.

- What do you mean?

- What's going on? You seem – different. To usual.

- Do I?

- Yeah. A bit. Distracted.

- I'm fine.

- No, you're not. I'm sorry about earlier I just . . . I'm trying to figure out what's up with you.

Silence.

- Suppose I have been a bit distracted. Out of sorts. Moody. Grouchy. Quiet. Too loud. Testy. Touchy. Eating more than usual. Eating less than usual. Can't stop buying stuff but I don't want anything. Can't focus. Get obsessed. Overwhelmed. Worried. Watch myself from above. But I don't feel sad or angry or anything at all. Bored. And empty. My heart is made of thin fibres, that feel like they could snap.

- What did you say?

- Just that I think I've been out of sorts.

- Maybe you're feeling a bit lonely?

- What?

- Do you think you're – lonely?

- I'm not lonely. I've got tons of mates.

- Loneliness has nothing to do with being alone.

- You think?

- I know.

- You think I'm lonely?

The animal howls again but it feels further away this time. The performer takes a moment to acknowledge the sound.

– Only you know if that's true or not. I'm just saying . . .

– Only sad people are lonely. Only sick people are lonely.

– That's not true. Everyone gets lonely.

– Then what is it?

– Loneliness? It's an animal. With two yellow eyes and paws like dinner plates.

– Scratching.

– It prowls quietly and pounces when you least expect it. Stalks in the shadows.

– Scurrying.

– With two yellow eyes and paws like dinner plates.

– Something behind me.

– Loneliness is an animal. That laps at the puddles of your patience. A tongue so wide and wild, it could wrap itself around you.

– It can sneak up on you for no reason.

– It will hunt you down when you're weak. It needs to feed.

– Loneliness is an animal.

– It cannot be tamed. But it can be sent away. So. Sprinkle salt in a circle. Say its name three times in a mirror. Set a trap bated with cold meat. Drop a net from above. Buy it a one-way ticket to the other side of the world. Change the locks.

– Scratching.

– Scurrying.

– One foot in front of the other.

–   Or just give it a name. Call it loneliness and know that it can be sent away. If you work at it, it can be sent away. But it does takes work and time or sometimes it's as simple as looking it in the eye and naming the animal so you can send it away.

–   Just give it a name.

–   And work at sending it away. You see if you're feeling like this again, you'll just – say something. Or at least – give me a hint. Because trust me – we've all been there and there is no need to feel so – alone in your loneliness. And I know it's not easy, but at least try and say something. Promise?

–   Promise. And I think I will go to bed actually.

–   That's probably not a bad idea. It's amazing what daylight can fix.

–   Yeah?

–   Yeah.

–   Yeah.

–   And next time you feel like you're lost in a forest. Tell me.

–   Okay.

–   Promise?

–   Promise. Hold on how did you know about the forest?

–   Scuff the mud on the floor that becomes the carpet that becomes floorboards that becomes foundations that becomes the ground again.

–   The trees become leaves become patterns on the wallpaper, becomes the forest again.

–   The swirls on the ceiling become the sky, becomes the ceiling again.

–   A world covering a world covering a world.

–   One foot, then another.

–   One foot.

–   Then another.

The end.

Ozymandias
by Jack Nurse
& Robbie Gordon

Ozymandias *was created in collaboration with young people through the Royal Conservatoire of Scotland's Widening Access to the Creative Industries Department including Cameron McHugh, Roisin Barry, Jack Stewart, Kara Louise Cassells, Piotr Janski, Stevie Michaela Differ, Gregor McMillan, Molly Bryson, Sean Russell, Aidan Kerr*

Writer's Note

This play is a story. A story to be told by a group. Each line of text is narration, and every new line indicates an opportunity for a new speaker. When a line starts with a dash – this indicates a line of dialogue by one of the characters: Joe, Alex, Sharon or Tattie and all the others we meet along the way. Important note for casting: Alex is a female person of colour; Joe is a white male and the rest is up to you. Feel free to change any other characters' pronouns.

One

We are in a grand, oak church.

It's over 200 years old.

Perhaps.

It's changed uses over the years.

Changed contexts.

From religious building to a community centre to what it is now.

Not a church but.

A pub.

A pub in a small town.

It's one of a number of pubs that exist in a chain.

I won't name the name of that chain because I personally don't want to endorse it in this play.

That's not what this play is about.

This play is about a plan that has just been hatched.

A plan that is muddy and muddled.

And doomed from the start.

But it is beautiful.

A beautiful plan.

Hatched during a global pandemic.

In a pub that's only just reopened.

That will serve anyone.

Literally anyone.

Including seventeen-year-olds Alex and Joe.

Who have hatched this plan.

The plan.

On the evening of exam results day.

Alex is sitting at a table in the pub.

She's like a deer with an afro in a pair of scuffed Reeboks.

And she's watching her favourite episode of *Breaking Bad*.

Again.

The one in the desert with the big gun fight.

Where one of her favourite characters dies.

One of the good guys.

Alex sighs:

– This world isn't fair for the good guys.

Joe is facing a plaque at the back of the pub.

He is a pint sized wildcat in second hand Doc Martens and an army jacket.

With a red sharpie in his hand like it's a bloodied weapon.

The plaque is so shiny he's able to see his own reflection.

He loves this.

And he starts to draw on the plaque.

A small diagonal line.

Joe draws another line.

Joe writes the letter Y.

Joe writes the word 'YOU'.

He writes 'YOU ARE KILLING PEOPLE BY DRINKING HERE'.

He writes 'YOU ARE KILLING PEOPLE BY DRINKING HERE AND YOU HAVE THE BLOOD OF MIGRANTS ON YOUR HANDS'.

Alex is still at the table.

There's a pile of torn up beer mats next to her pint.

It's a guest ale and this one is murky.

Treacly.

And a bargain at £1.49 a pop.

Last night, Alex watched the film *The World's End*.

Where the characters go on a pub crawl.

Called the Golden Mile.

But this is the only pub in town that will serve them.

The Steampacket.

Because the bouncers.

Pete and Vic.

Who look like a pair of stoned Highland cows.

Can't count or read so they don't ask for I.D.

So for Alex's version of the Golden Mile with Joe.

They are making their way through the guest ales instead.

Three down.

Two to go.

Tattie is meant to be here too.

But he's late.

As always . . .

In Scotland, Tattie means potato by the way.

Aye it does.

In Scotland, aye means yeah.

Aye that might come up a lot during this.

Joe is still at the back of the pub.

He takes a photo of his work to show Alex later.

But there's nothing mighty about scribbling on a plaque.

It isn't enough.

So he begins to pull.

And pull.

And pull.

His grip tightens around the frame.

His rubber soles start to slide on the carpet.

But nothing's happening.

He clenches his teeth.

As his fingers start to bleed:

– This'll show Alex. 'Oooh I'm Alex and I'm going to study film at uni in Edinburgh. Oooh Edinburgh.'

Unaware of what's going on at the back of the pub.

Alex is still watching *Breaking Bad* on her phone:

– You're the smartest guy I've ever met but you're too stupid to see he made up his mind ten minutes ago. Do what you gotta do . . .

BANG.

And in that instant, someone who was once great became nothing.

Just left standing there in the middle of the desert.

Gets Alex every time.

Except this time.

Because she's not really focusing on *Breaking Bad*.

She's tearing up another beer mat.

Thinking about how Joe always thinks he's right.

About how smug he is:

– 'Ooh I'm Joe and I'm going to study politics down the road because I'm so woke.'

Alex doesn't care.

Doesn't care about anything.

Not anymore.

Not after today.

She's got her hood up, arms folded, buried in her phone.

Now, this isn't how you would usually act in a pub.

You wouldn't usually tear up beer mats or watch TV on your phone.

You wouldn't usually drink the £1.49 guest ale.

And you definitely wouldn't do all of these things together.

And Pete the bouncer notices all this.

He may not be able to read or write but damn he is perceptive.

Perceptive Pete.

Perceptive Pete also clocks the braces on Alex's teeth.

He clocks her school leavers' 2020 jumper.

And he clocks that Alex must be underage.

When there's a crash from the back of the church.

Joe is lying on the floor.

Plaque still intact.

When he is dragged away by the scruff of his neck by Vic.

Quite viciously.

Vicious Vic.

– You work for him, you're complicit! You're COMPLICIT.

Joe shouts, clutching the sharpie in his hand with pride.

And Vicious Vic grunts:

– Just doing my job, wee man.

And all the badges on Joe's army jacket glint in the light.

Extinction Rebellion.

Amnesty.

Black Lives Matter.

You name a cause.

He's got the badge.

The badges glint as he's dragged outside.

He takes a seat on the curb outside the pub.

As Alex bursts out the door behind him:

– Fuck this. Fuck this pub. And fuck this town too.

She sits down next to Joe.

She actually puts her head in her hands and says:

– The only thing to do now is the plan.

The plan was only concocted on round three of the guest ales.

It was never something she had thought about doing before.

But she is so frustrated.

With everything.

It feels like it's the only thing she can do.

Alex and Joe both say:

– That was your fault.

They're in the huff.

Just as Tattie walks round the corner sniffing a pound coin he's found to check if it's real.

Tattie's like a giraffe, a really thick giraffe, in a yellow chequered shirt.

He comes to stay in the town every summer.

With his gran.

When his parents take their annual seven-week holiday to Marbella.

They're fuming they've only just got away now though.

And their seven-week trip.

Will only be three.

And they'll have to quarantine for two weeks when they get back:

– Bloody Europe.

Tattie always gets left behind because it's cheaper.

But he doesn't mind because he likes his gran and he likes the guys too:

– Sorry I'm late guys. Guys?

– We're barred.

Alex is livid:

– Barred from the only pub in town that'll serve us.

And a really clear idea forms in Tattie's head:

– Do you get barred from a bar cause it's like . . . a bar?

Alex rolls her eyes:

– I can't wait to get out of here.

Joe can't help but mock Alex:

– Yeah everything will be sorted when you go to Edinburgh. There's no problems in Edinburgh. Oooh Edinburgh.

Tattie smiles:

– You got the grades you needed then?

Alex nods vigorously:

– Yeah. Yeah. Obviously I did. Yeah.

And Joe's buzzing 'cause he's got the grades to go to uni just outside of town:

– It's only one bus and, get this . . . my brother reckons I could get away with paying a half fare because I could pass for sixteen and the bus driver's sound.

But Tattie's not been as successful.

He's not been successful at all.

It's fine though:

– I'm going to go work with my Uncle on the farm anyway.

Tattie wonders what they're going to do if they can't drink.

He wonders what else there is to do.

In this town.

On an evening like this:

– So what's tonight all about then guys? Guys?

Joe's mood changes.

He looks nervous.

Tonight, he's going to need to put his money where his mouth is:

– We have a . . . eh . . . a plan. You know that statue in the town centre?

Tattie doesn't:

– Aye, of course!

Alex looks Tattie dead in the eyes:

– We are going to steal it's head. And chuck it in the sea.

Two

We are outside a DIY centre.

On the outskirts of town.

It's big.

It's orange.

And we won't name this one either.

It towers over our heroes.

Heroes?

Not quite.

Not yet.

Joe is leading the group into the shop to get their supplies.

For the plan.

The big orange shop is closing at ten.

And it's ten to ten now.

So they've only got ten minutes.

And Tattie's like:

– What's the plan again? Guys?

The plan is to tear the head off the statue.

To steal it.

To decapitate it.

And throw it in the sea.

They know it's possible.

Because when they were in first year the rugby team nicked it.

And had a game with it.

Joe remembers how the boys who stole it were treated like heroes.

Absolute legends.

And about how much of a statement it made.

But Alex is remembering how much it hurt people in the town.

People crying over a silly statue.

And she thinks if they're going to get that upset about something that isn't even alive.

They deserve to be upset.

The automatic doors of the big orange DIY shop swing open.

Alex and Joe stop dead in their tracks.

Like they've seen something genuinely terrifying:

– Fuck.

They dash behind an empty transit van in the car park.

Joe whispers:

– It's her.

He's freaking out.

The whole plan is unravelling in his head.

He can't face this.

Not now:

– What are the chances of her working here?

Why does it have to be her?

Tattie's not been listening because he's now licking the pound coin to see if it's real:

– Who? Guys?

Joe murmurs in a hushed horror:

– Psycho.

The last person you'd want to have to deal with.

At a big orange DIY store.

At 9.50pm at night.

When this person is the only one serving customers.

Psycho is a girl who was in the year above them at school.

But, they never talk to her.

Not anymore.

They never even look at her.

Tattie wonders why she's so scary:

– She's just a lassie.

– That's actually quite sexist.

Joe says as he gazes down at his #metoo badge.

Alex rolls her eyes.

And tells Tattie ominously:

– She was the school discus champion.

Fear begins to grip Tattie.

Joe makes her out to be the Boogeyman.

Alex is more specific:

– John Wick. The Baba Yaga. The person you send to kill the fucking Boogeyman.

Tattie's bricking it.

But Alex keeps going:

– Darth Vader. Sauron. She's fucking Sauron.

Tattie's confused:

– Sharon Pyscho?

– Sauron. Sauron the Dark Lord of Mordor.

– She's a murderer?!

– Kind of. She used to be in some of our classes at school but she's into some really dark shit and she's a proper weirdo. We need to go home. Tonight isn't the night.

Alex butts in:

– No tonight is the night!

And Joe can't.

He's too nervous.

Alex calls him a shitebag.

Joe hates being called a shitebag:

– Well if I'm a shitebag. Well you just think you're better than everyone else in this town but . . . eh . . . you aren't.

– It's hardly difficult to be better than everyone else when this is where you live.

– Well you won't have to deal with it come September, eh?

– Aye. You're right.

– Good.

– Sound.

– Fine.

– Cool.

Tattie hates fighting.

Especially when it's between the only two people he's ever come close to calling pals.

In this town.

So he shouts:

– Are we going to steal this head then?

– Ssssssshhhhhhhhh.

Alex focuses up:

– Yes. But we need to avoid Psycho at all costs. So . . . you have to go Tattie. I'm sorry. I would if I could. You'll need to take one for the team. She can't do anything to you. She's working in a shop. There would be too many witnesses.

Tattie goes:

– Nah.

And Joe's like:

– Do you want us to die Tattie?

– Nah.

Alex concocts a very clever plan:

– Well, we'll flip for it. Fair is fair. Heads I win and tails you lose.

– Sound. Does seem fair.

Tattie loses the toss.

Obviously.

And Joe gives him his shopping list.

One.

Big.

Fuck.

Off.

Rope.

And tells him:

– At all costs tell no one the plan! Get in. Get out. No fucking about.

Alex smiles:

– Thanks Tattie this really means a lot to us.

But Tattie's just desperate to have mates here.

Otherwise it will be a very long few weeks at his gran's.

A long few weeks drinking tea.

And watching EastEnders.

So Tattie runs into the shop.

Like a soldier going into battle.

Not 'cause of the plan.

'Cause he's bursting for a piss.

Tattie's in front of the toilets.

Pulling at the doors with both hands.

They're locked.

Remember what Joe said.

Don't reveal the plan.

Get in.

Get out.

No fucking about.

Psycho sees Tattie.

She eyeballs him.

From behind a Perspex screen.

She's like a caged grizzly bear in a Fred Perry polo shirt and an orange apron.

She's furiously chewing chewing gum.

Masticating as if it's a threat.

Like how dogs bare their teeth to fend people off.

She is.

In all honesty.

Very scary:

– WHAT DO YOU WANT?

She puts on her mask and stalks across the shop.

Towards Tattie.

Maybe she is aggressively flirting with him?

And Tattie thinks:

– Is she flirting with me . . . little old me . . . little old Tattie?

No time to think about that. Get in. Get out. No fucking about.

The piss situation has become critical.

Tattie runs towards Psycho and asks her for a rope.

Psycho growls:

– What kind of rope?

He starts to describe the rope he needs.

But it becomes a how long is a piece of string.

Well, rope.

Kind of conversation.

He says it needs to be big.

And long?

And thick?

Yeah thick.

– Hyp-er-thetically . . . it would need to . . . let's say . . . kind of wrap round, like, a neck . . . ? Aye. A neck like my neck. Aye it needs to tie around a neck and kind of like hold the weight.

He demonstrates the action of tying a rope around his neck.

The desperation of needing the toilet is at an unbearable intensity.

He looks really on edge.

His bladder has gone solid.

Like glass.

And tears fill up his eyes.

As a single tear droplet falls down Tattie's cheek.

Psycho grunts:

– Are you fucking alright?

Tattie needs to get out of here.

He starts to back away.

He clocks a rope on a shelf and grabs it:

– I'm sound. Long night. Didn't get my results. Going to work with my uncle on the farm. It'll be sound. Been to the pub. Never got in. Mates got kicked out. Got a plan though. Fuck. Wasn't meant to mention that but aye!

He doesn't realise he's nearly out the door with the rope in his hand:

– Know what I mean?

Psycho is looking at him like:

– The fuck you on about?

As Tattie dashes out the shop for a piss.

Alex and Joe are waiting in the car park:

– Yas Tattie!

He runs towards them.

They seem genuinely thankful.

That he went in instead of them.

They're happy, even, to see him.

It almost feels like they are about to hug.

Which they've never done before.

Four arms outstretch towards Tattie.

Waiting for an embrace.

That never comes.

Because Tattie bursts between Alex and Joe.

And pisses against the transit van:

– Aaaaaaahhhhh!

The piss splashes back all over his trousers.

All over the shoes of Alex and Joe.

And all over the rope.

– Shit.

The rope.

Tattie hasn't paid for the rope.

Which is still in his hands.

Just as Psycho appears at the entrance.

Like an animal stalking her pray:

– OI! GET BACK HERE NOW!

But she's actually trying to help.

She has just seen a boy with tears in his eyes brandishing a rope.

Around his neck.

Like a noose.

So she's decided to run after him.

To stop him.

But all Joe sees is Psycho running towards them.

He punches Tattie in the arm.

Grabs the rope off him.

Gives it back instantly.

Because it stinks of piss.

And just when they thought all was well.

When the plan seemed like it was on track.

They start to run:

– Tattie what the FUCK have you done?

Three

We are running.

Running.

Running past council houses.

Posh houses.

Beach.

And grass.

Running through the town where Joe and Alex grew up.

It's just like your town.

You'd probably hate it.

But when people visit they say it's nice.

Even if they don't mean it.

Psycho is hot on the heels of the team.

She can't understand why they are running away.

So she starts to speed up and shout after them.

But it sounds like a roar.

Tattie repeats the phrase:

– I don't to want to die.

– I don't to want to die.

– I don't to want to die.

– I don't to want to die.

– I don't to want to die.

It feels like we've been running for miles.

– She's like the fucking Terminator.

Alex shouts as she gasps for breath.

She's absolutely gubbed.

Having spent most of lockdown on her couch watching films.

Psycho's not very fast.

But she was the school discus champion.

So she has stamina.

It feels like she could run forever.

It's like a fucking horror film.

Tattie's not ran in ages.

He'd forgotten how good it feels.

He's smiling.

Holding the stolen rope.

Running with his mouth open.

Like a Labrador.

When he swallows a cloud of midges:

– Eurgh.

Joe is focused.

Fired up.

The plan is coming to fruition.

He knows that this is what he needs to do if he wants Alex to see things differently.

Even if Psycho is hunting them.

Alex is given some energy by thinking about the weight of what they're doing.

The gravity of the situation.

How much people love this statue.

And how she's going to fuck it up.

No one cares in this town.

About anything that matters:

– Especially not me.

And she's going to break one of the silly things they do care about.

To show them.

Show them how stupid it is.

Joe hurtles down the country road.

He thinks of all the people throughout history who have inspired him.

Who have done something significant.

Changed the course of history.

All of the people that have come before him.

And led him to this moment.

Martin Luther King.

Ruth Bader Ginsburg.

Clement Attlee.

AOC.

Neil Armstrong.

Rosa Parks.

Mandela.

Ghandhi.

Thunberg.

Obama.

He wants a seat at that table.

He wants to be remembered for doing something.

Something good.

A political act that he believes will set him on the path to greatness.

Just in time for studying politics at uni down the road.

That'll show Alex.

Tattie's in his own wee world.

He's the most relieved man on the planet.

The weight of mother nature has been vanquished.

Never again will he feel such a burden on his bladder.

The price for this is soggy smelly shoes.

But he doesn't notice this as he runs.

Runs.

Runs.

Straight to the town square.

Some steaming guy hangs out a pub like a sloth and shouts:

– Run Forrest run!

Alex loves that.

It's just what she needed.

She picks up the pace.

And as the group turn a corner.

On to the high street.

She slips on the tarmac.

Her hands and wrists taking the brunt of the impact.

Her jeans ripping as they scrape the surface.

Joe and Tattie stop and look back.

Psycho is standing over Alex.

Her prey at her mercy.

Alex shouts at the others:

– Go on without me! Finish the job we started!

Joe hesitates at a crossroads.

Literally.

– We can't go on without you . . .

Alex stretches out her blood-stained hand and points:

– GO. Go on. I'll be fine. What we do in life . . . echoes in eternity.

Tattie's jaw drops:

– Man that's like . . . Shakespeare.

Joe shakes his head:

– It's fucking Gladiator. Come on. Let's go.

So Joe and Tattie run.

Run.

Run away.

Leaving Alex and Psycho as two tiny dots in the distance.

Four

We are still on the tarmac.

Achy knees.

Stinging hands.

Out of breath.

Alex has been left behind.

She's back where we left her.

On the ground.

Her hands are cut.

Full of gravel.

Psycho looming over her.

She doesn't know what's going to happen.

And then . . .

Psycho offers her arm to Alex.

And helps her.

Helps her?

Psycho helps her up.

Alex shouts:

– Get off me and get back!

She begins to back away slowly.

But Psycho just stands there looking.

Looking at her.

– Stay back. Or I'll scream.

Alex reckons this situation is the opposite of Jurassic Park.

Where the advice is to just stand.

As still as possible.

Until the velociraptor goes away.

But Alex can feel the pain in her bloody and bruised knees.

She can't run.

Even if she wanted to:

– Fuck this. Fuck you. And fuck this town. Why does nothing ever go to plan?

Psycho thinks this is very rude.

She's only trying to help.

And she doesn't understand why Alex is swearing at her:

– What the fuck's wrong with you?

– I'm pissed off.

– How?

– Do you know what day it is?

– Eh, Tuesday?

– Yeah, it's Tuesday but it's also . . . exam results day.

– Ah . . . And you're pissed off cause . . .?

– All I want to do is leave but I can't. I'm stuck here with people like you. People like Joe. In this stupid town.

– People like me? You better watch what you're saying.

– People in this postcode like you who did shite in their exams and didn't get out of here. So the powers that be have decided that because generations before me did shite in their exams, I've done shite in my exams too.

– Doesn't mean you have to be a dick about it. I never gave you your exam results.

– All that hard work, months of graft, hoping that for just once things would fall my way, and my results aren't even based on what I've done, but on this fucking town.

Then suddenly a skulk of tracksuit clad lads who look like foxes come screaming around the corner.

The ringleader is bouncing a Fevernova football.

Beating it against the ground.

Like a drum.

Their high-pitched giggles fill the empty street:

– Aw Psycho. Please don't batter me!

– Aw Psycho. Please don't eat me alive!

– Aw Psycho. Please don't kill me a with a discus like you killed that PE teacher!

Psycho roars.

Hoping they'll scatter.

But the foxes just get louder.

Giggling and squealing:

– Goth.

– Emo.

– Devil worshiper.

– Goth.

– Emo.

– Devil worshiper.

– Goth.

– Emo.

– Devil worshiper.

Alex thinks this feels like watching a fight where someone's on the ground.

But the other person just keeps kicking.

Kicking.

Kicking.

They're not stopping.

Hurling insults.

But Alex recognises one of the foxes.

Wee Grant from next door.

Hood obscuring his face.

But it's hard to be anonymous.

When you're wearing a big massive puffer jacket.

An orange big massive puffer jacket.

That your mum bought you.

So you don't get run over.

Wee Grant only gets a new jacket once every three years.

That he's made to grow into.

Shame this one is brand new.

He looks like a baby fox poking its head out of a big orange sleeping bag.

So Alex shouts:

– Wee Grant. Your mum still writing your name inside your coats, aye?

The squealing turns inwards.

As the foxes' attentions.

Turn to wee Grant.

As if he's a chicken in foxes clothing:

– Let me see your label.

– Nah.

– Mummy's boy.

– Loser.

– Virgin.

– Wee balls.

– Runt.

Wee Grant squeals:

– NAH FUCK YOU. I'M GOING HOME AND I'M TAKING MY BALL HOME WITH ME.

And the foxes chase him up the road.

– Cheers.

Psycho's actually just thanked Alex.

She was polite.

And never grunted.

Or growled.

Or roared.

Alex feels guilty now.

For saying the things she's said about her.

And for running away.

Alex can't even remember Psycho's real name:

– Psy – Pys –sorry . . .

– What you sorry for like?

– Erm . . . nothing?

– Why were you running away then?

– We were running from . . . you.

– From me . . . ?

– Aye. I guess that's why I'm sorry. We are – were – I know it sounds silly – scared of you.

But Psycho isn't worried about that.

She's worried about Tattie:

– Where's the boy?

– What boy?

– The tall one. Kind of thick looking. Long neck. Bit like a giraffe.

– Tattie?

– We need to stop him from doing something stupid. Something that he'll regret.

– Fuck sake. Did he tell you the plan?

– Well it's kind of obvious isn't it?

– What?

– Boy comes in, crying, talking about how he needs a rope that'll wrap around a neck and hold the weight? It's hardly rocket science.

And Alex realises that the reason Psycho has been chasing them.

Is more than just a stolen rope.

She has been running after the group.

Not to hurt them.

But to save Tattie.

And Alex thinks it's like Psycho's got superpowers or something.

But she never got bit by a spider.

Or came to Earth on an asteroid.

She's just sound.

That's her power.

Psycho kneels down and tightens her laces.

Ready for another sprint.

Like the seasoned athlete she is.

– Wait.

Psycho looks up at Alex.

– I promise you that Tattie is OK. I don't know what he's said to you. But he got the rope for us. Me and Joe. We've got a plan and it's not what you think. You've got the wrong end of the stick. We're going to . . . eh . . .

– Going to what?

– Eh . . .

– C'mon spit it out.

– Steal the head of that statue in the town centre and chuck it in the sea, alright?

And Psycho starts to laugh.

So hard she gets that funny feeling.

In her belly.

Like she's been doing sit ups.

Training for her next big discus competition:

– So you're taking the statue down as revenge?

Alex nods.

And Psycho gets it:

– That's a pretty fucking neat idea man. I hate this place too.

– Na. It's a daft idea. I'm done with it.

– Aye it is daft. But cool though.

– You're actually quite nice.

– Quite? You seem surprised.

– When tonight is over with you should come hang out with me and Joe sometime.

– Joe's a prick.

– Aye. He is.

– I don't do that kind of thing anymore anyway.

– What . . . friends?

– Aye. I like being alone.

She smiles at Alex:

– Let's go.

Five

We are in the town centre.

With Tattie and Joe.

Tattie is crying.

Inconsolable tears.

He's using the end of the stolen rope as a tissue.

Forgetting its covered in piss.

He's just watched his mate be consumed by an actual psychopath.

He's thinking of all the scary films Alex has made him watch over the years.

Every summer.

Since he was far too young.

The Demogorgon.

The Babadook.

– Hannibal Spector.

And Alex is the one that dies first.

She doesn't deserve to.

She's one of the good guys.

And Tattie cries:

– You are so mean Joe. You don't care about anyone else apart from yourself. You left her to DIE.

Joe's adamant:

– We're here because I care.

The sky is pitch black.

There's an orange flicker from the streetlights.

And there's no one around.

Apart from . . .

A silhouette that casts a long shadow across them.

Joe points to it:

– We're not leaving without his head. For Alex.

Tattie's gaze follows the shadow upwards.

It leads to a plinth.

Which leads to two bronze feet.

Up to two bronze legs.

Up to a bronze body.

Up to a bronze head.

The statue in the town centre.

The statue that's stood there for years.

The statue they've always known was here.

But never really looked at.

It's part of the walls.

Part of the furniture.

You don't even notice it when you walk by.

Because it's always.

Just.

There.

You've probably got one in your town too.

Big.

Metal.

Inoffensive.

Except Joe thinks that it is offensive.

He's read it somewhere on the internet:

– See this. See what this represents. Imagine being Alex and walking past this every day. Imagine walking past this symbol of racism. And . . . hate. And . . . eh . . . oppression.

When you're just wanting to go to the shops for a sausage roll and a can of Vimto.

Tattie's bawling his eyes out now:

– You don't care though. You don't care about him or us. Alex loved Vimto and you left him be eaten by a psycho.

Joe grabs Tattie by the shoulders:

– We are here to . . .

– OI!

Psycho bounds around the corner.

The neon glow of the Chinese takeaway sign behind her.

We won't name this one either.

Well we probably could cause it's not a chain like Spoons or B and Q.

Fuck.

Anyway, the neon glow is behind Psycho.

It makes it look like she's teleported there.

Like one of those science fiction films Joe couldn't name but Alex could.

– AAAAAHH PSYCHO!

Joe and Tattie scream.

Alex is with her.

– Run Alex! Get away whilst you still can.

And Tattie starts swinging the rope around his head.

Like it's a lasso.

Whilst letting out a high-pitched scream:

– She'll fucking eat you!

But Alex is calm.

And tells Tattie:

– This is Sharon.

Tattie's confused:

– I thought you said she wasn't called Sharon Psycho?

– No . . . she is actually called Sharon. Just Sharon.

Tattie's brain melts a bit.

But Psycho, sorry . . . Sharon.

Sharon has picked up on her nickname:

– Why you calling me Psycho like?

Everything goes quiet.

It's tense.

And then . . .

Inevitably.

Tattie vomits words:

– Well Alex and Joe say that you're pure weird and mad and
that. And that you're a murderer. Is that right? Did you guys
say she murders people and that? Guys? Aye I think that's
what they said. Oh, and you're quality at the discus. Oh oh,
and they say you stab yourself because you don't feel pain.

And each negative comment.

Each bit of rumour.

Chips Sharon's armour away.

Chip.

Chip.

Chip.

She's not a grizzly bear anymore.

She's a teddy.

She looks . . . surprised.

Shocked even.

Like . . . devastated.

She turns to walk away.

But Alex shouts:

– Wait. Stay.

They sit on a bench overlooking the sea.

Tattie stays standing.

He is still so scared of Psycho.

SHARON.

Sharon explains.

She explains why people are scared of her.

She explains the truth.

Her dad died.

People started to act like she didn't exist.

Because she was sad all the time.

She took a few months off school to get better.

That's it.

– Shit.

– People are scared because they don't understand.

Or maybe don't want to understand.

Sharon shows loads of tiny white lines on the pink skin of her forearm:

– No one would talk to me when I went back to school.

She looks at Alex and Joe:

– You used to at least say 'hello'.

Joe looks down at his Samaritans badge.

He knows he's been a dick.

But this is the first time he's heard it.

The first time he's had to face it.

We're in school now.

About a year ago.

In a classroom.

It's like a zoo.

We're sitting in dark brown plastic chairs.

Eyeing up Sharon's bag when she says she needs to go to the toilet.

Joe waits til she leaves.

Grabs the bag.

And chucks it out of the window.

– Yasssssssss!

– Quality!

– Absolute legend!

He feels like a hero.

He's always wanted to be a hero.

The bag is lying spilled open in the playground.

Everyone is laughing about it.

You're laughing about it.

Until Sharon walks back in.

Now our heads are down.

And we are sniggering into our jotters.

Joe is terrified of what the consequences might be.

What might happen to him.

He's shiteing himself.

Waiting for a reaction.

Waiting to see what she might do.

But she doesn't do anything.

She's just sitting there really quiet.

Not saying a thing.

And in the town square.

This fear of Psycho.

This fear that's turned into knowing who Sharon really is.

And what she's going through.

It's all too much for Joe:

– You all need to get a grip! Alex let's do what we came here for. Tattie hand me the rope. We're here to do a job.

But Alex is done.

Done with the plan:

– Let's go home.

– But . . . I'm only here for you.

– I don't want to do it anymore.

– I want to do this for you.

– It's not going to help anything.

– I know what it must feel like for you to walk by that every day.

– What are you talking about?

– The statue.

Joe flashes his badge of a clenched fist:

– 'Black Lives Matter.'

– That statue is of Robert Fucking Burns. You know that, right?

– Exactly. He was a slaver.

– You're a fucking slaver.

In Scotland, slaver means someone that salivates.

Like what they're saying isn't true.

Or grounded in fact.

As in:

– You're talking shite. He accepted a job on a Jamaican plantation, but he never went.

Joe realises that his knowledge of Robert Burns doesn't extend past the headline of a *Guardian* article.

– Joe . . . if I wanted to make a political point about race, I'd go tear down a statue of an actual fucking racist. And maybe I will when I get up in the morning. Maybe it'll be a thing. Me. The Statue Destroyer. Like Indiana Jones but better. Because the chance of doing what I actually want to do has been taken away.

– What do you mean?

– This town has taken away my opportunity. Fucked my chances of getting out of here.

– But you are getting out here, you're going to Edinburgh?

– Na I'm not.

– So you're going to stay here with me? That's brilliant. Why?

– They never gave me the grades I deserved. So I can't leave this town. That's why I want to hurt it. 'Cause it hurt me.

Alex looks up at the statue:

– And this town fucking loves this thing. They hold festivals about it. Read his shitey poems. Mention it at any available opportunity as if it means something. And this town, this town that fucked me over, would be gutted if they woke up and it was missing. That statue represents someone that had the chance to get out of here and do things with his life but I don't have that chance.

– But why do you need to get out here? Come with me to uni. It's only down the road. And it's easier to get in. We can still be friends.

– We're not friends. We've just grown up in the same place. Went to the same nursery, same primary and same high school. There's six billion people in this world and you're the person I'm closest to in a town of 14,000. And I don't want to go to the shitey uni down the road, that's not the point.

Joe looks down at his badges.

Looking for answers.

But there's none.

He's crestfallen:

– I thought this is what you wanted. I thought this was . . . like . . . getting it right. I thought this was being your mate.

– Well treat me like a mate then. Like you would everyone else. I'm just a girl. A person. Doing a thing to prove a point. Like loads of other teenagers have done before me and you're just making this about something it's not because of who I am. If you're here for the colour of my skin or the badges on your jacket then you're here for the wrong reasons. If tearing down statues is a symbol of chucking out old ideas and a sign that times need to change then – you know what – that is what I'm going to do. In the name of all the people that got fucked over today. That's exactly what I'm going to do.

Alex takes the rope off Tattie.

Ignores the pungent smell of piss.

Climbs up on to the plinth.

Wraps the rope around the neck of the statue.

Holds on as tight as she can with both hands.

And . . .

Jumps.

But . . .

The statue doesn't move.

Obviously.

It's a statue.

It's made of bronze.

So Tattie runs up behind Alex:

– I'll help you.

And Sharon swaggers up:

– I was the school discus champion, I'll get this thing down no bother.

Alex glances at Joe:

– Come on.

And if this had been last week.

Or five minutes ago.

Even thirty seconds ago.

Joe would've thought that this was his moment.

Claimed the idea.

And looked down at his Black Lives Matter badge.

With false pride.

But he realises it's not about that.

It never has been.

It's about Alex.

It's about his mate.

And his job is . . .

To give space.

Share space.

Step aside.

And fucking listen.

He takes his badge covered jacket off.

And tosses it to the side.

He looks at Alex and nods:

– For you. And nothing else.

Six

They grab onto the rope.

Like a shambolic tug of war team.

But they are not the only ones performing this action.

Somewhere Medieval Christians are smashing sculptures made in Ancient Rome.

As the team begin to pull.

And pull.

And pull.

Somewhere in Copenhagen someone writes 'racist fish' on the statue of a mermaid.

As our heroes' grips tighten on the rope.

Somewhere a gang break into a crypt and steal an 800-year-old head.

As the rubber soles of their trainers start to slide on the tarmac.

Somewhere only the boots of a Russian dictator's statue are left.

As the statue in our story begins to move forward.

Somewhere a Spanish conquistador destroys an Aztec temple.

As Alex.

At the front of the queue.

Shouts back:

– It's starting to give!

Somewhere workmen take down a statue on behalf of the local council.

As the statue begins to buckle.

Somewhere a group of US soldiers facilitate tearing down a statue of a dictator they killed.

As it begins to crack.

Somewhere there is a group of young people similar to them pulling down a statue of a former slave owner in Bristol.

As it begins to bend like it's made of something that is not metal.

Somewhere the Taliban destroy a statue of Buddha.

As Tattie's lip begins to bleed.

He's biting it hard from the effort.

Somewhere a statue of Christopher Columbus falls from the sky.

As Sharon glances at her bicep and thinks:

– I could throw the discus for Scotland.

Somewhere at a flat party a Catholic burns a tenner and shouts:

– Fuck the queen.

As Alex searches for a film reference but there is no film as cool as this.

She looks behind.

Smiles at Joe.

Turns back to the front.

And inhales the magnitude of this moment:

– For everyone that was fucked over today.

Somewhere Robert E. Lee hits the deck.

Somewhere Hafez al-Assad hits the deck.

Somewhere Adolf Hitler hits the deck.

Somewhere Jesus hits the deck.

Somewhere King George III and his horse hit the deck.

Somewhere a new statue is placed upon an old plinth.

A statue that speaks to today.

That speaks to now.

But it might not speak to tomorrow.

As Joe shouts to the team:

– It's almost there!

And the statue bends to a ninety degree angle.

And there's a horrible sound.

Like a wounded monster.

As the bronze becomes detached from the knees.

And our statue.

The statue from this story.

Hits.

The.

Deck.

So that only two trunkless legs remain.

And the rest of the broken body lies.

On the cold hard concrete.

Tattie shouts:

– This is an act of historical poetry guys! I thought we were only taking the head.

And our heroes embrace.

For the first time.

Their job is done.

As the sun emerges above the furthest hill.

The night turning to day.

A new dawn settling on this town square.

This toppled monument.

On these people.

Tattie.

Sharon.

Joe.

And Alex.

They are just like you.

Just like me.

Just like us.

And they turn to one another and they say:

– What next?

End of play.

Next

There's a lot of different reasons why statues get pulled down.

Alex says:

– Tearing down statues is a symbol of chucking out old ideas and a sign that times need to change.

If you think times need to change then here's something you can do.

- Look into news stories regarding the tearing down of statues.

- Do your research (unlike Joe). Research statues, street names and landmarks in your area. See if you can find any problematic history associated with them or anything that needs to change.

- Write a letter to your local MP and demand action.

- Feel free to write as individuals, in pairs or in small groups – whatever suits how the research unfolds.

- You can use these letters to end this performance, if you like.

- Make political noise.

Bad Bored Women of the Rooms
by Sabrina Mahfouz

Writer's Note

Things in (brackets and italics) *are optional directions for the individual groups to add if appropriate for their group and sometimes to include their own writing – it can be a few seconds or a few minutes or it can be left out.*

Words in italics *in the text are to do with mixology, they can be spoken by a specific performer playing the mixologist or shared out as wished.*

All other directions and the distribution of the lines are at the discretion of the company.

Prologue

Here we are.

In a room.

A bunc(h of self identifying young women.

(and allies and non binaries and . . .)

(In separate rooms we should also say.)

Being women.

You know how The Woman Song goes . . .

We are strong.

We are brave.

We are born leaders.

We are fierce.

We are not to be underestimated.

We are enough.

We are beautiful.

We are powerful.

We are unstoppable.

We are incredible.

We are talented.

We are –

blah blah blah

we are flipping bored.

There's not a chorus that could

communicate our discontent sufficiently.

We wanna cause some mischief.

We wanna dance on bartops

with or without tops on

we wanna rob a bank

and get away with it

so we wouldn't have to sit here

day after day thinking about which grant to apply for,

which job might last past a recession.

We wanna rip down the walls

hiding hallways of hapless politicians

and just take over,

start over,

bulldoze their basicness

into a renewable energy resource

to light up our new world,

alongside the raging fires that fuel us

and burn us and drain us and char us.

We may be enough

but we have had enough

of strong and brave and beautiful

being enough.

We want to be

criminals.

We want to break every single law

laid down to make life limp.

We could be good, we could be the best

and it would NOT pass the power test.

Cos look at who we have in Westminster?

Look at who is taking the piss out of our laws

and our good, clean thoughts every single day?

Nah, if that's how we have to roll to run things

we're game.

We always have been.

Women are not just mums and daughters and sisters.

We are motherfuckers too.

And we're coming for you.

Rooms & Crimes & Women & Drinks

Hi!

We are the bored women of the rooms.

(*Performers can intro themselves – by their real name or a character name. They can add details or just names – or not!*)

Joining you from our rooms in 2020 (*change as necessary*).

Rooms date back to at least 2200 BC,

excavations on Santorini have shown

early Minoan structures with clearly defined rooms.

But if you believe that a tomb is a room,

a room for your deathbed basically,

your forever room,

then they've been doing those in Ireland since at least 3600 BC

and then of course globally.

So basically, there has been a lot of rooms.

And a lot of women.

An estimated fifty-four billion women have existed on this planet

since the beginning of time.

And there's around 3.5 billion women on this planet right now.

And each of them goes into a room at some time,

even if it is not 'A Room of One's Own'.

Rooms have always had women in them.

Imagine!

There was probably never a room

that a woman hasn't been inside.

Even the ones they still aren't allowed inside,

like some in London's Pall Mall members' clubs,

they probably still clean them

or deliver something to them

or pick someone up from one of them.

Unless it is a whole guarded peninsula,

like Mount Athos in Greece

where there are thousands of rooms

for thousands of men across hundreds of kilometres.

But women are completely banned.

Though, you know, so are FEMALE ANIMALS

– neither can come within 500 metres of the coast.

Unless the female animal is a cat.

Pussies are okay because they catch the many mice

that would otherwise eat all the food.

The plus side of this no female animal except cats thing

is that it makes being vegan very easy.

This is Greece, by the way,

not some far away place

that gets some good old European funding

to tackle its gender discriminatory policies.

The only women who have entered

the Mount Athos peninsula have done so illegally.

Starving raiders in the Greek Civil War who stole flocks

that were allowed to roam there during the conflict.

Dressing as a man got a few in and that resulted

in the maximum twelve month prison penalty

that now exists for any other

criminal woman

who might try it.

Criminal women.

In prison, some of them, some of them not.

Some of them in prison for crimes they didn't commit,

or did commit

but if they did then 80 per cent of those crimes are non-
violent and mostly shoplifting, theft or fraud offences –

the very thing the people at the top

of our power structures, be it in business or politics,

are experts at,

so stealing without the protection of the law

is pretty much what they are locked in those rooms for,

away from families and children and jobs and hobbies

and loves – rooms where they are needed

and that do not cost the public

an average of £37,543 per year to lock.

Some criminal women have never been caught by the law
and strangely or not so strangely

haven't been caught

by the global imagination industry either.

Not given much thought,

not many books, hardly any films –

comparatively, anyway.

Think about Al Capone, the Krays, Pablo Escobar – criminals
more famous than fairy tales.

We're not including serial killers here,

though all these lot had bodies that added up, sure,

but it's more about the empire they built illegally,

against the norms of society

but in the same way the normalised empire builders

did too – just one was posh and the other wasn't.

The murder parts were to keep being able to commit

the crimes they committed without being stopped

or caught or killed themselves.

Which is not an excuse, they're still killers,

but they are criminals first, not the other way round, which
is maybe semantics

but it's the bit we're interested in.

Where are the women like this?

Not in the top ten Google of famous criminals

that's for sure.

Bonnie gets a mention, Clyde adjacent of course.

Which is not insignificant.

That the only women criminals that are household names
are the ones who worked out their criminal crossword
worlds with their intimate male partners.

Those with husbands, boyfriends, lovers –

the men who were really in charge of course.

These women might be allowed to get famous,

for being so naïve as to fall for the persuasive,

perverted powers of a man bent against society's norms

rather than for any ingenuity or lawless ferocity

of their own.

And we just think, and yeh, maybe it's too many hours

spent on Zooms in our rooms drinking Rosé,

but our thoughts on this are simply that

if we don't recognise the bad shit,

the fact that women since time immemorial

have been motherfuckers too – for money, for power,

for fame and without any moral awakening at the end,
without any baby to protect or wrong to avenge

– though is that really possible for a woman in the end? –
Well, if we don't at least recognise the first bit

about women being motherfuckers too

then we can't possibly get recognised

for the normal, boring things we do,

like –

(*Add in things the performers have done in their rooms over lockdown that they are genuinely or ironically proud of or are totally mundane but still a success considering our situation – show if appropriate!*)

for example.

So we wanna raise a glass to some criminal women.

We have cocktail makers

– *mixologists as we like to be called* –

making, mixing cocktails to raise to these criminal women.

And by drinking them down

we hope to

get drunk and less bored

yes but also, to remember, they were there

we are here

and in the rooms of power criminals roam

stealing from the people, doing such worse things

than what these women did,

so with every sip,

which does not have to be alcoholic,

we hope you remember this too.

Griselda Blanco

Griselda Blanco

– 50ml blue agave blanco tequila –

was a major cocaine dealer in Miami

– 15ml fresh lime juice –

becoming one of the biggest drug dealers

in the Western hemisphere during the 1970s and 80s

– 20ml wine syrup.

She invented the motorbike drive by killing

but used any method going to get rid of enemies

that seemed the slightest hindrance,

250 such people legend has it,

including three of her ex-husbands.

She got one of them and six of his bodyguards

with an Uzi in a nightclub car park,

after he betrayed her on a deal

– 20ml beetroot juice.

She spent nineteen years in American prisons,

Twenty-three hours in a 4x4 room

that's 131,765 hours in a room,

before being deported back to her original home

of Colombia

– 15ml orange juice –

where she was shot in the street,

ironically by the very drive by bike-killing she invented. She
was carrying £150 worth of meat from the butchers and a
Bible under her arm

– 3 salt flakes.

Put all the ingredients in a shaker.

Shake with cubed ice for six seconds and strain into a tall glass.

Finish with a lime twist.

What was she doing, with all that meat?

The Bible?

Feasting?

To remember those she'd killed?

Or to forget them, blood blanked by blood?

Offering sacrifices to the statues of Catholicism,

repenting flesh with flesh?

'Tonight, we will feast.

Pray to the Virgin Mary

for her blessing

and we will sing

the names of those we've killed.

It will be a long song.'

Maybe she was cooking for the homeless,

distributing pork chops and sirloin steaks to the streets

as she preached her favourite passages from Genesis –

but see, there we go, giving her a redemptive ending,

when men who've killed so many for their cocaine thrones
need none do they?

So no.

She stays there, dead on the stone by rival gangs,

covered with meat she was going to eat herself,

or feed to the young men she paid

to bathe her in rose water,

using the Bible to make them pledge allegiance to her

until death.

Yes.

It tastes good.

– *The La Madrina*.

Nesmut

Next. Number two.

– *One metal chalice*.

Ancient Egypt, the place beer was invented

– *200ml brown ale* –

and an Ancient Egyptian woman called Nesmut.

A leader of tomb robberies in the Valley of Kings

in the Twentieth Dynasty

– *one teaspoon of honey*.

Not much else is known,

but we can suppose that as this much is known

she was caught and it was recorded

and perhaps she faced the same sentencing

as other women who were caught for conspiracies

against the powerful men who kept them in a harem – nose
and ears cut off

or, as a special treat, invited to commit suicide.

It was a time of minimal crime, supposedly.

Or things seen as crime now weren't then, who can say?
They did consider tomb raiding the very worst crime –
higher than murder even,

to plunder the sacred resting room of the greats.

So it is likely she faced death.

Decapitation, drowning, being burned alive

– 50ml extra smoky whiskey.

Combine all the ingredients in a cocktail shaker and fill with ice.

Stir this mix gently for ten seconds

and then strain into the metal chalice.

Before this though, Nesmut led the way

through those limestone tombs,

marble room after marble room,

masterful at trickery,

architecturally telepathic,

unmapped mazes unphasing to her strong eyes and arms,
holding a lamp in one,

removing stone with another.

To eventually, stealthily, successfully

steal the gold and emeralds of kings and queens –

until of course the day she got caught and recorded,
allowing us to know this,

which begs the question how many other

women criminals of history are untold

just because they were too fucking good at it?!

Plus we could probably add all queens

to the criminal category too,

depending on your politics,

which we don't have enough alcohol to discuss today

so nothing to fear,

we'll leave them alone for now

and allow time to judge or atone

their ways of accumulating their wealth,

whether it was stolen back by women like Nesmut or not.
Bottoms up!

– *The Tomb Raider*.

Madame Ching

Number three. Ching Shih. Madame Ching.

Terrorised the China seas in the 1800s

– *2 drops of poppy seed tincture*.

Has appeared in bit parts on screen,

including Pirates of the Caribbean.

But here, she is solo. Leading alone.

As she did back then, with 40,000 men,

women and children under her unforgiving wing.

The most successful pirate in the whole of history

– *50ml dark rum*.

And never caught.

Fought the British, the Portuguese

and the Qing Dynasty

– *3 peeled and de-stoned lychee fruits*.

Her rules were strict and cruel,

though sometimes pretty good it could be said.

No pirate was to steal from any villages that sold them
supplies.

Pirates who raped female captives were beheaded,

YES,

but then consensual sex meant death for both parties,

legs wrapped with cannonballs and thrown overboard,

any disobeying at all of the rules

meant head chopped off too so . . . you know

– *25ml sweet and sour.*

She started her career as a sex worker

and at twenty-six married a notorious pirate, had two kids

and when her husband died five years later,

took the whole enterprise over

and expanded it to the be the force

that only the Portuguese could eventually get to surrender
years later, when Ching hung up her eye patch,

opened a brothel and married her adopted son,

having two more kids with him, in her 40s.

We have been told so very many lies, haven't we?

– *25ml cherry brandy.*

Combine all the ingredients in a blender and blend thoroughly.
Shake with ice and strain into a Martini glass,

garnishing with a slice of lime.

What did she do with all that money?

Made on the back of beheaded necks

and young girls having sex with whoever could pay?

She must have made sure she gave plenty of it

to her family,

they were all around her bed at home when she died, crying,
crying for this criminal woman,

their mother, their friend.

What would they spend it on?

This one is strong.

– *The Ching Cherry Martini.*

Marion Boyd, Countess of Abercorn

Marion Boyd had nine children

who survived childhood in sixteenth century Scotland,

so that was pretty good going.

Maybe she thought it was luck

or maybe she thought it was the double power

of Protestant prayer from her husband,

James Hamilton, Second Earl of Abercorn

who did a lot of Irish colonising for King James,

and her own Roman Catholic counsel,

unusual pairing for the time and perhaps this is why,

as thanks for the nine surviving,

she promised her priests she'd raise her kids Catholic.

– *This one is non-alcoholic. Ironic, yes.*

Blind eyes were given to this wish until her husband died.

Then, she was excommunicated

from the Church of Scotland and locked up

in Edinburgh's Tollbooth cells for two years

as an uncharged criminal, awaiting charges

for believing in the same God

but differently.

– Take time to make your own Irn-Bru Simple Syrup

by pouring a can of Irn-Bru into a pot,

warming it through on the stove until it reduces to a syrup consistency,

then chill.

Two years it took for the laws to decide

there wasn't a charge to be made

and the cells were needed for witches and whatnots

so she was put on house arrest at home in West Lothian

to make sure she didn't sneak out to meet Catholic priests,

who had to keep things under wraps

but were not under house arrest themselves.

She died soon after she arrived.

– Half a shot of ginger and lemongrass cordial.

A criminal woman without being charged of a crime.

Detention without trial,

it's still all the rage right now of course.

I hope for that time Marion couldn't leave the house

she found a room with a window

overlooking the green slopes

and spotted orchids of Duntarvie,

maybe asking a remaining child
to pick some to put in a vase so she could see them
even when it got dark outside,
with their pink or purple spots
and stripes on their three-lobed lips.
Perhaps she imagined walking
in the sharp, fresh air without a guard
and when she knew she could not ever do so again
she struck the cone-shaped cluster of spiked flowers
to her heart and made its chambers split apart,
to escape room after room of nowhere to go,
to finally flow freely through Scottish hills
and castle walls –
but who really believes in ghosts?
Shake the shot of Ginger and Lemongrass Cordial
and half a shot Irn-Bru syrup over ice.
Strain and serve in a Gimlet glass. Marion's Mocktail –
might be one of your five a day.

Linda Calvey

So finally. Death. The Black Widow,
as Linda Calvey has been nicknamed
– *75ml black vodka*.
East London born and bred,
a loving 1950s Stepney childhood,

working on the Roman Road market

selling wigs with her mother

till she fell in love with a bank robber,

married him and lived happily till

Linda was tipped into getaway driving

after her husband was shot dead by police

during a botched bank robbery job

and soon after she was the one with the guns out

and doing the getting, not just the getting away

– plenty of ice.

Vodka, lime and soda was her favourite drink

after a hard day at work

– 5ml fresh lime juice –

bursting through heavy doors to demand bags

filled with cash and rings and all things sellable

– 1 teaspoon edible pearl dust.

She tells it better in her book.

Written this year, after eighteen-and-a-half years

in a prison cell for murdering her then husband, apparently

– 5ml Simple Syrup.

Shake all the ingredients together.

Add extra pearl dust to the bottom of a coupe glass

and strain cocktail into it, stirring

or adding more pearl dust if needed for shimmer.

She denies it. The murder of him.

Not her life of crime,

of leading armed robberies around London,

of being proposed to by the men who did what she did

but whose names go down in history-

Charlie Bronson, Reggie Kray –

saying no thanks, doing things her way.

This drink's for you, sip it slow, *The Black Widow*.

And so what about us, now.

You?

Still in our rooms.

Still unsure of what we can do that is really a crime

or not really a crime in the eyes of ethics only politics

or a crime that would get some of us punished

and others of us celebrated.

Yep.

But at least now we are a bit pissed

or high on halal fizzy Haribo

or the meditative melody of proper green tea

whatever is your fix, your thing

we have been here to bring you

what we brought you –

dubious drink recipes

and a gaze –

a bored women in a room gaze

on other women who were doomed

by the sort of world we say we don't want

but we still build.

Who were mostly,

except our Scot, obviously

NOT VERY NICE WOMEN,

if you add everything up but then who ever does?

It's confusing as fuck.

But we still got stuff to celebrate, right?

Like –

(*Performers add in here things to celebrate*

about their lives, futures, hopes – real and/or ironic/dreamworld.)

So we celebrate through the confusion

to find a way through to some sort of truth,

we hope we told it how we could.

Pass it on,

slan ge var.

The End.